THE DEAD GOOD
FUNERALS
BOOK

Sue Gill and John Fox

Engineers of the Imagination
Ulverston, Cumbria, England

ISBN 0 9527159 0 2   Paperback

Formal Disclaimer

This book is a guide to choices and should
not be taken as a complete or authoritative
statement of the law in England and
Wales. Whilst every care has been taken
with the content of this book, the authors
and publisher cannot be held liable for its
accuracy. Neither the publisher nor the
authors of **The Dead Good Funerals
Book** can accept responsibility for any action
taken as a result of reading this book; the
reader would be wise to get a second opinion
or to consult professional advisers.

Published and Distributed by,
and available from
Engineers of the Imagination
Welfare State International
Lanternhouse, The Ellers
Ulverston, Cumbria
LA12 0AA
01229 581127
info@welfare-state.com
www.welfare-state.org

also
Edge of Time Ltd
07000 780536
sales@edgeoftime.co.uk

Printing
Finger prints
Unit 44
Trinity Enterprise Centre
Furness Business Park
Barrow in Furness
LA12 2PN
01229 432959
info@fingerprints.co.uk
www.fingerprints.co.uk

Typesetting,
Design and Layout
Jonathan How
Coherent Visions
BCM Visions
London WC1N 3XX
0870 444 2566
design@coherentvisions.com

To Ken West MBE for his inspiration and generosity

ACKNOWLEDGEMENTS

The process of writing this book has been like building a cairn. Many people have contributed a stone along the way. We would like to thank them all and in particular: Gilly Adams; Steve Andrews; Rosie Bell; Natasha Bradshaw; Martin Brockman; Pete Brooks; Tom Brown; Naheed Cruickshank; Jean Grant; green fuse; Rev Canon Bill Hall; Mrs Sheila Hall; The Funeral Standards Council; Elaine Harrison; Rose Heatley; Help the Hospices; Roberta Hopkins; Hilary Hughes; Professor Malcolm Johnson; Maria MacLachlan; Cara Mair; Caroline Menis; Jane Milton; Lorna Moone; Pete Moser; Fiona Ogilvie; Stephanie Wienrich at The Natural Death Centre; Once; Richard Osborne; Sheila Page; David Penn; Rosetta Life; Hazel Selene; South Shropshire District Council Environmental Health; Jane Spottiswoode; Catriona Stamp; Peter Stark; Rev Geoffrey Steel; Paul Swift; Tate, Liverpool; Clive Tempest; Trinity Hospice; Patrick Upton; Mike White; and Ann West.

Special thanks to Dot Queen whose unbelievable good nature saw her through the typing of every draft and endless revisions, Jonathan How for his stoic patience and Refkah A'Court for her tenacious research and revision for the 2004 edition. We would also like to thank Arts Council England, North East and Arts Council England, North West.

We would like to thank the following for permission to reproduce from their publications: Harper Collins Publishers Inc for the poems "Late Fragment"; "No Need" from **A New Path to the Waterfall** by Raymond Carver (1989) and for the poem "Our Greatest Fear" from **A Return to Love** by Marianne Williamson. Hodder & Stoughton Ltd for extracts from **Funerals and How to Improve Them** by Dr Tony Walter (1990), Spike Press for the poem "Goodbye" from **Waiting Women** by Pauline Prior-Pitt (1989), Brian Patten for his poem "So Many Different Lengths of Time" from **Armada Flamingo** (1996), Roger McGough for his poem "Defying Gravity" from **Defying Gravity**, Penguin (1993), Bloodaxe Books for the poem "The Minister" from **The Collected Poems 1955-1995** by Anne Stevenson (2000), John Fox for his poems "Secular Prayer" and "Holding On" from **Ground**, Engineers of the Imagination (1998). The front cover picture shows the work of Duncan Copley. Woodcuts throughout the book are by Martin Brockman except that on page 66 which is by John Fox. Every effort has been made to trace the copyright holders of the poems published in this book. The editor and publisher apologise if any material has been included without permission or without the appropriate acknowledgement, and would be glad to be told of anyone who has not been consulted.

CONTENTS GUIDE

LATE FRAGMENT

Raymond Carver

And did you get what
you wanted from this life, even so?
I did.
And what did you want?
To call myself beloved, to feel myself
beloved on the earth.

PREFACE

Most of us wish to find the best way to live our lives. Marking and celebrating significant moments of change or loss can be important stepping stones.

For many years Welfare State International has been creating secular ceremonies to mark rites of passage, initially for birth and welcomings, then partnerships. In the 1990s our work extended to mark death and remembering. Usually, these ceremonies have been on a personal and domestic level.

The work has evolved and unfolded into a richer and wider perspective, including many more points of transition that our society has previously ignored.

Our belief in the importance of this work has led us into finding a way to put it into the public domain through publications, exhibitions, workshops and training courses, as well as continued face to face practice as celebrants and funeral officiants.

Our rites of passage programme at Lanternhouse offers opportunities to many participants: to students, an MA in Cultural Performance with Bristol University; to artists, occasional commissions to make new work for use in real ceremonies; to organisations, a service of public

**Welfare State International
Engineers of the Imagination**

Founded in 1968 by John Fox, Sue Gill and others, Welfare State International is an arts company based in Ulverston, Cumbria at Lanternhouse, its award-winning Centre for the Celebratory Arts. After gaining a world-wide reputation for creating celebratory events with communities and for pioneering prototypes of site-specific events such as lantern festivals, carnival bands and fireshows, the company has turned its attention to vernacular art. We are seeking a culture which may be less materially based but where more people will actively participate and gain the power to celebrate moments that are wonderful and significant. This may be building our own houses, naming our children, burying our dead, announcing partnerships, marking anniversaries, creating new spaces for secular ceremonies and producing whatever drama, stories, songs, rituals, ceremonies, pageants and jokes that are relevant to new values and new iconography. This work is documented in Engineers of the Imagination (Coult & Kershaw), Methuen, reprinted 1992, and Eyes on Stalks, John Fox, pub. Methuen 2002.

ceremonies for significant occasions; and to individuals who wish to become freelance secular celebrants, workshops and summer schools for training and professional development, led by Gilly Adams and Sue Gill.

In extending and examining our own practice, as part of the Year of the Artist we invited international artists to turn their visions towards funerary objects and artefacts, which resulted in the DEAD exhibition at the Roundhouse, London in 2001.

For Great Ormond Street Hospital for Sick Children we steered a public requiem in 2001 for many hundreds of bereaved parents who came together for a Ceremony of Remembrance.

Art can have a particular role in helping us to come to terms with the complexity of death. Some artists, writers and musicians offer insight through their work and bring to the surface the unmentionable, the unspeakable. On a simpler level, the aesthetics and craft of presentation, architecture and funerary objects can improve an ill-considered ceremony.

The Dead Good Funerals Book is not an academic text. It combines research with first hand narrative and complements important publications like the New Natural Death Handbook which contains impressive lists of resources.

In 1996, when the first Dead Good Funerals Book was published, we took a somewhat hectoring tone on behalf of the bereaved, directed at funeral directors, local authorities, education authorities, the NHS, the Home Office and the Church. It is heartening to be re-writing this introduction seven years later since huge distances have been covered by the funeral industry, and public interest and demand has grown for wider choices. We can confidently report that, although a little nudging is still necessary, the glass is no longer half empty, but most definitely more than half full, bubbling with pioneering ideas and approaches to what makes for a dead good funeral.

FOREWORD

The last years of the 20th century were marked by a growing public interest in funerals. As people became aware of the options, and as more options became available, resistance grew to the impersonal standard package or assembly line approach in favour of something more personal and hands on.

The AIDS epidemic was influential in the late 1980s as many young people affected by death wished to make the funeral a personalised event and had time to plan for it. In 1990 Tony Walter's book, Funerals and How to Improve Them, raised a theme which seemed to reflect a concern already felt in some quarters. Certainly the next few years were marked by a flurry of initiatives addressing it. The Natural Death Centre was established to help people arrange inexpensive, Do-It-Yourself and environmentally-friendly funerals. The British Humanist Association's manual Funerals Without God and its training of officiants made it easier for people to have non-religious funeral ceremonies. Burial in a natural burial ground became an option when Carlisle City Council opened the first in 1993. Welfare State International brought the perspective of artists and specialists in ritual and in 1994 ran a series of weekend courses. Its Guide first appeared in 1996. This decade also saw the launch of the National Funerals College by the great social entrepreneur Michael Young, publication of the Dead Citizen's Charter, the establishment of the Heaven on Earth coffin shop in Bristol and the appearance of a small number of alternative coffin manufacturers and funeral directors.

Almost all these initiatives came from creative and socially aware people outside the funeral industry asking themselves how funerals could be improved. Virtually the only insiders who contributed to the movement were those running the country's cemeteries and crematoria who adopted the pioneering Charter for the Bereaved formulated by Carlisle's former Bereavement Services Manager, Ken West, MBE.

The reformers and their organisations often seemed wacky at first and the notion of individuals wishing in whatever way to challenge the norm met with short shrift from the majority of funeral directors.

But by the year 2000, when a figure as celebrated as romantic
novelist Barbara Cartland was buried, according to her
wishes, in a cardboard coffin under her favourite oak tree,
and mourners each threw a handful of earth into her grave
to the soundtrack of Perry Como's ballad I Believe, the tide
had obviously turned. Nevertheless it wasn't until 2003
that the funeral establishment finally acknowledged these
developments when the British Institute of Funeral Directors
mounted what they (wrongly) believed to be the first ever
exhibition of coffins and caskets for the public together with
English Heritage.

One of the main problems in organising a special funeral
is that unlike life's other major ritual event – the wedding
– most people do not wish to plan ahead. But a funeral that
is out of the ordinary needs vision, imagination, confidence
and preparation. Even with all the recent changes, timely
information and guidance is not always easy to find. This
new updated Guide offers an excellent planning companion
whether your need is immediate or whether you would just
like to inform yourself in preparation for that unknown date
in the future.

Rose Heatley

What is a Funeral?

A funeral says that there has been a death. One particular life has ended. It marks the value of one life that has come to an end, through a gathering. People come together to pay their respects, to mark the passing of a loved one and to take their leave. The funeral requires them to hand over their loved one and begin the process of separation. A funeral is a life issue.

There are many wise and sensible laws and regulations concerned with death, dying and disposal of the body. We have to encounter these, and satisfy them all before a funeral can take place. There are good leaflets from the Department of Social Security and Age Concern, for example, to tell us what we must do and how to find our way through the maze.

- There are laws that say we must obtain a Medical Cause of Death Certificate.

- We must register the fact that the death has occurred.

- Whether we choose to dispose of the body by burial or cremation, the correct procedures must be followed.

- Staff in local cemeteries and crematoria can advise free of charge on these procedures.

- Public cemeteries and burial grounds keep meticulous records of where the grave is and who is in it.

Then there is the funeral to arrange. How soon should it be? Where and at what time? Who should care for the body in the meantime? Should it be burial or cremation? (70% choose cremation) Will there be a service? Who is going to lead it? Should a coffin be used and if so, what sort? Where can we buy one? Does religion need to be involved?

We need a transport plan; bearers for the coffin; a catering plan; an accommodation plan for distant relatives. We need to let people know the arrangements, and decide whether to put notices in the press, handle scores of telephone calls.

This is usually a public event and needs to be managed, so that it goes off according to plan. Afterwards, there may be a memorial to choose and/or charitable donations to administer.

Deciding how many sandwiches to make or what colour the flowers should be gets mixed up with the official paperwork; worrying about paying the statutory fees in time gets mixed up with deciding whether the young children should attend or whether all the family have got something suitable to wear. They are quite separate issues. Some are mandatory duties over which we have no choice, and other decisions are purely personal. There seems so much to do and so many decisions to make.

So this is where the undertaker or funeral director comes in. Someone who knows the routine inside out, particularly the complications of negotiating with a hospital or dealing with the coroner in certain cases. Professional help and guidance, when we are upset and find it difficult to cope, seems exactly what we need. A godsend, some would say.

It's a difficult time. Articulate and creative people whom we know found themselves, after the deaths of elderly parents, "in a state where we couldn't muster even friends." So what about the untimely death of a partner?

There is no such thing as a right answer. If we come from a position of celebrating or marking other important life events – births, marriages, divorces, redundancy, death – maybe we can begin to articulate feelings of bereavement and find symbols, actions or rituals that resonate. A funeral needs to be seen as an extended experience, with several occasions for paying tribute to the dead and marking our leave-taking, not only in the twenty minutes allocated in the crematorium, but over the days, weeks and months to come and in different settings: in the home before the funeral, in the church, during a favourite walk taken later, over a special meal ...

Organising a funeral is not easy, but it is possible, particularly if it has been given some thought before the death. The DIY funeral would certainly not be right for most people, but we are not advocating that the choice is between doing the whole thing yourself, or handing over 100% to a funeral director. There are paths forward between these two poles, which need clarity and firmness, but which offer a more satisfying outcome.

The Dead Good Funerals Book

How artists got involved with funerals

We held our first weekend on "Funerals and how to make them more personal" in 1994 and it was packed to capacity. Enquiries from Brazil via Heidelburg, media interest from Johannesburg to New Zealand, meant that we had to turn many away.

It was an extraordinary cross section of people: landscape architect, clergymen and women, academics, arts workers, nurse, HIV/AIDS counsellors, crematorium manager, PR officer for an undertaker, environmentalist, lesbian and gay bereavement project workers, psychotherapist, midwife, hospice workers, many of whom had come with both personal and professional agendas, but all with an interest in DIY funerals of one sort or another.

Meeting Lorna Moone, an arts worker from the North East was more than we had bargained for. It emerged early on that her son Danny, 25, had died less than a year ago, after mental illness and 'six months in a kind of coma'. There are two reasons for devoting a passage of this chapter to Lorna. Firstly, the detailed order of service, all the music, poems, stories and readings at her son's funeral, were carefully documented and she gave us copies, with three written pages of afterthoughts. Secondly, there was a strange personal resonance. Our son Daniel is the same age; he has the same name; only he is very much in the world. An abyss separated us, and I struggled to reach across to this courageous woman who had decided to come along. Lorna wrote:

> "It was a gruelling six months, but I did have a chance to give a lot of thought to the whole business of funerals. In a weird sort of way, focusing on his funeral helped me. I was determined that it must be very different from any that I had previously attended.
>
> I think it worked. It did what a funeral should do. (It took place on the day that would have been his 25th birthday).
>
> Tony Walter's excellent book **Funerals and How to Improve Them** changed many of my ideas.

Our biggest problem had been deciding where to have the ceremony. My ideal would have been a forest clearing or an empty beach – but you do have to think of things like access by elderly relatives as well as giving some consideration to their beliefs. A room in the pub or the community centre didn't feel right either. I wanted a spiritual place – but I'm not a Christian.

In the end we settled on the church. I had honest talks with the vicar about my vague beliefs or lack of belief and he was willing to compromise. He gave a very good address. We had talked a lot about what he should say. I was anxious that mental illness and suicide would be talked about honestly, but also very sensitively, bearing in mind that some in the congregation would be schizophrenia sufferers.

I was glad we took up the vicar's offer to have the coffin brought to the church the previous evening. I felt more ready to face the next day. The first sight of it was like a kick in the stomach. It helped to "do things" that evening. We draped it with a banner, arranged lots of big jugs of garden flowers all round it and left a candle to burn overnight (the banner had previously been made, not for this purpose, but with a very close group of women friends, and it seemed right to use it ...).

At the service, I didn't feel able to read my own poem, but it did help having things to do again. I lit a candle for the start of the service. I would have liked to have involved more people doing things."

Music included Bob Dylan's "I shall be released", Missa Luba, an African Mass. There were original poems, Danny's own story read from a letter to a friend."

Lorna regretted the seating, and only noticed too late: family and friends in the first few rows, other people respectfully filling up from the back, with a definite gap. She would have preferred a circle.

Photographs need careful thought. By request a friend discreetly took some (without using a flash). This upset

Lorna's daughter when she saw them. She really wished they had not been taken.

A saxophone played as young friends, with Danny's sister and brother, carried the coffin from the church in procession to the cemetery, prior to the reading from **The Prophet** by Khahil Gibran. At the graveside Lorna hated the plastic grass, regretted she had not made more arrangements herself, like organising a team to fill in the grave, rather than just wandering off, leaving it unfinished. Having a book at the reception in the pub after was a good idea. Lorna thought people would just sign their names, but as the wine flowed, the book got filled with messages to Danny. Lorna values that book very much.

Our son Daniel is a musician. A few weeks before the Funerals Weekend he had composed a suite of music, for an entirely different context. It contained a haunting anthem and I had taken a tape of it with me to the Funerals weekend. It was a gift for Lorna.

Whose Funeral is it?
Understanding and Planning

There is quite enough pain around death and dying without adding more for the bereaved through anxiety about making suitable funeral arrangements. We leave our families with a burden when there is no understanding of what we should like to be done after our death or how it might be done. Discussion, planning, preparation is not macabre when we are alive, and when we are dead it's too late. Sudden, unexpected or premature death is the exception. Most people die nowadays at the end of a period of ill health or when they have reached an age at which death might be expected. Family members would feel more certain and comfortable and better able to express a clear choice to the funeral director, if there has been a degree of preparation. If we can begin to cope a little with the subject of death, which in a world of uncertain beliefs has become a taboo subject, then it makes it easier for others when it comes to start arranging the funeral. This is a time when we are often in a confused state, suffering from shock, despair, guilt, self-reproach or even disbelief.

So, tread carefully. There are really useful services to be

bought from funeral directors, such as dealing with the statutory authorities, to save our energy, time and attention for personal details. But it seems we have to be alert enough to opt out of those parts of the standard funeral package that we don't want or that seem inappropriate or downright distasteful. See **Embalming** for example.

Many managers of Cemeteries and Crematoria, we have found, are delighted to be consulted. They are longing to be asked what services they can offer. A direct meeting is far more likely to result in getting the timing of the funeral to suit you. In most cases they do not meet the family until the cars draw up at the crematorium, or at the grave side, and then it's too late to change any arrangements. Too late to turn off the taped music or to substitute a personal choice, too late to rearrange the chairs, too late to get rid of the plastic grass at the graveside, too late to fetch four or five more shovels to fill in the grave. Time and again they would be pleased to do whatever they can to make sure people get whatever arrangements are right for them. Our advice always is to start with these people – they can often provide many more services and guidance than the public think. They can certainly provide a wealth of advice and local information.

There are more choices and scope around funerals and memorials than most people think. You do not need to have a funeral at all. If you do, it does not need to be in a licensed building – a small funeral could be at home, for example (unless you want an Anglican service in England). You are not required to use a clergyman. You are not required to use an undertaker. Legally, you are not required to use a coffin (but frequently local by-laws say you must if you want to enter an official cemetery or crematorium). Your burial may be on private land; you may be buried under a tree in your garden for example.

The first decisions you need to take are regarding:

■ cremation or burial

■ if burial, conventional or natural

■ if cremation, what is to happen to the ashes

■ religious or non-religious ceremony

- all or partly DIY

- what material is the coffin

Once you know what route you wish to take, you can start the planning. Bearing all this in mind may help with making

---

Home Burial

To arrange a burial on private land, that is not an official cemetery, you should begin by consulting the Environmental Health Officer at your local district council. Law and local policy differ in this area and only they will be able to give the specific information required. South Shropshire District Council have published a very clear and helpful leaflet to guide people in that particular area through the process. The contents, however, are the opinion of one local authority and individual local authorities should be consulted in each case.

Their guidelines raise various issues and pointers including:

- That the grave needs to be at least 100 metres from a borehole, well or spring, 10 metres from a ditch, drain or watercourse.

- It is advised that the burial is marked on the property deeds and that the local police and council are informed to prevent potential future problems.

- Although rare, checks should be made to ensure there are no by-laws or covenants preventing burial on that particular piece of land.

If guidelines are followed, burial on private land should not present any problems.

'I have advised about twenty persons over two years regarding private burial, many of whom decided to use green burial sites as the most practical way forward that fitted their personal requirements (South Shropshire has two green burial sites). I also surveyed and assisted in the practical location of 4 private burial sites locally. There seems to be a greater desire from many people nowadays to be associated with a scene or landscape which they hold dear to themselves rather than a particular church or cemetery. What seemed to help the individuals and families most in each of these circumstances was the clear knowledge of the wishes of the individual. People also expressed the desire for friends, family and descendants to know something about them from the place they chose.'

Richard Osborne
South Shropshire District Council

---

some choices and in feeling some ownership of the funeral, although that is said with caution. A funeral must be about beginning to let go and not about achieving some private agenda or clinging to unfulfilled hopes for the person who has died.

Recommendations about planning and information are not an endorsement of pre-paid funeral plans, which get presented as a solution to part of the problem. While they are mechanisms for dealing with financial anxiety, they will become a reactionary force inhibiting change or a re-look at the way we think about funerals. As a legal contract of service, with specified details, that is going to be entered into and signed up maybe thirty years before it is acted upon, no-one will give authority to change any of the details when the time comes. The proliferation of these schemes will actively prevent change and increase fossilisation of the service. The fees exclude disbursements – costs over which the funeral director has no responsibility – and which are therefore excluded from the promised package. As these can add another 30% to the bill the family can still be in for a shock. And finally, as the supreme example of Pay Now Die Later, tying up all that money so far in advance has the industry laughing all the way to the bank. Changes in consciousness might encourage people to plan in advance and might allow that to be perceived as helpful not morbid. The lady on the cheese stall in our weekly market, having seen my photograph in the local paper with a painted coffin said:

> "I think it's good; these things should be more in the open, more talked about. After all, just because I make a will, it doesn't mean I'm going to die".

... A nice thought, but sadly, oh yes, you are. She is going to die and so am I, so we might as well recognise it.

Some Funeral Practice

It must be stated that there is no legal requirement to have any kind of funeral ceremony at all, nor are there any statutes governing what form any ceremony should take. The law protects and gives certain rights to people who choose to be buried or cremated without the rites of the Church of England or indeed of any other church. It gives clear rights of free access to the churchyard or graveyard to people willing to perform this kind of ceremony. If you decide to have a funeral ceremony, you can nominate any suitable person of your choice to lead it for you. People attending a funeral in the churchyard or graveyard are expected to behave "... in a decent and orderly manner" and the usual powers existing under law "for the preservation of law and order" may be exercised. In unconsecrated land within public burial grounds, ceremonies of any religion must be allowed under the Race Relations Act 1976. If Church of England ministers conduct full Christian ceremonies in unconsecrated land, the law protects them from any penalty. This applies to fields and woods for example, provided the landowner agrees to the ceremony taking place.

Article from The Scotsman by Audrey Gillan (Sat 23rd April 1994)

The rake pulls and scrapes, grinding along the worn brickwork, searching out the last piece of bone, some ashes, maybe a stray nail. Easing back and forward, the hand-wielded tool slowly gathers some last remains. The steady clank of metal hits the sides of the cooling oven, bringing its contents to a cooling box at its back.

Inside this oven, the heat can be anything up to 800 degrees Centigrade. Here, the flames consume flesh, hair, eyes, nails, even an artificial limb. This is the everyday reality of death. The clinical brutality of incineration, a side which we rarely bring ourselves to consider, let alone look at.

But here, peering through the glass doors of Carlisle Crematorium's three incinerators, is a group of people who have paid £98 to look death in the eye. Whether they fear it, or embrace it, they will walk in death's shadow for 48 hours. They have come to Cumbria to look at graves, coffins, body bags, ashes, urns and, more simply, to talk. Their concern is the funeral and how to make it more personal, interesting and human.

This is no return-ticket sojourn in the vale of tears, but a reaction against the compromised ritual that the modern funeral has become. This particular project has arisen from a desperate frustration with the services available, and a feeling that the business of death has become a monopoly. It has also grown from a realisation that death – and what happens after it – must be accepted so that we might enjoy life.

There in the clinical incinerating room the steel doors of the ovens, the gauges, the chimneys, the wheeled tables, the little drawers with their bags of grey ashes, the plastic canisters glamorously called "urns", prompt you to think you'll opt for burial, forget about the fear of the worms eating into your flesh.

The usual cremation time for a corpse is one hour and ten minutes. However, a body can take much longer to incinerate, depending on what has caused death. Women take longer than men because they usually have more fat to burn.

As he closes the door of the incinerator, the crematorium worker explains that the ashes are then placed in a cremulator, a steel drum with ball-bearings that pound them down through holes in its base. At the end of the process there are 2-3 kg of ashes.

"Personally, I don't want to go for burial in a kitchen flat-pack," jokes the silver-haired Bereavement Services Manager, Ken West, as he points to the pine-clad coffin, lined with pink and white satin. "How long do you think this lasts when it's in the ground? A year, a few months? Well actually it's just four weeks."

As he sighs, you can tell West's sentiment is at once spiritual and political. "If people knew what was happening to those coffins when they did a burial, I don't think they would be happy about it. But they simply don't know."

West has become so disillusioned by the British way of death that he has even devised his own wool shroud. Complete with wooden board for support and black cotton ropes it costs £85 plus VAT. He says: "I've been carried around by our staff in this and I know it works. It's our own design because we couldn't find a shroud anywhere."

Ken West explains all this as he walks proudly around his cemetery, through funerary glades, past carved headstones and along paths of mown grass. He laments the mown graves, condemning them as ecological deserts, continually trimmed by lawnmowers.

He guides you through each section of the cemetery, past vast Victorian monuments, through set-pattern graves to his new woodland burial site. Here, you can get back to nature and have a local oak tree planted on top of your buried remains. You squirm a little but the idea of giving something back to nature from the nutrients of your flesh appeals to you.

As the group walks among a patch of baby graves, past a collection of rattles, dolls and teddy bears, emotion suddenly crumples someone's face ... Gathering around him, the group explain to each other why they came. One wonders why the carvings on gravestones are so anonymous, tell you nothing about the person at all and more often than not use a name that the person was not known by, James instead of Jimmy, Dorothy instead of Dot.

These people have travelled from Edinburgh, Glasgow, Peterborough, Clwyd, all over to get together and discuss their notions. Some of them are women still traumatised by the experience of their children's funerals.

They are from all walks of life. Arts development worker, ministers, students, counsellors, undertakers, the owners of a private crematorium and people who are just interested. Ron Dick, a Church of Scotland minister, Jane Millard, a chaplain with the Episcopalian Church, and Lynda Grant, an arts development worker, work at Milestone House, the Edinburgh hospice for those suffering from the AIDS virus. Each has faced frustration with funeral traditions but has found that things can be done differently. Rev Millard says she is here to find a language other than words, that will help express people's hopes and aspirations as well as people's grief. "Very few of our folk are religious," she says. "So we try to listen and pick up what their spiritual symbols are."

At the many funerals at which they have officiated at Milestone, they have let off dozens of balloons at a funeral, they have made death masks, videoed funerals and found numerous other ways of carrying out appropriate celebrations of life. "I have stuck wheels on a coffin and pictures of Concorde," smiles Millard.

"Our job is also about helping people to realise that their life is valued, even if it is coming to an end. Most of the people at Milestone have crossed the frontier that many of us don't have the courage to contemplate: they must look at death and consequently have the time to plan its every detail. The situation produces ceremonies that are more interesting and personal," explains Lynda Grant: "A lot of our people who die are so young, they are prepared to do things in a different way."

These three feel they have learned a lot from their 48 hours at Carlisle. "We will be going back with a wealth of ideas," says Millard.

OUR DEEPEST FEAR

Marianne Williamson

Our deepest fear is not that we are inadequate, our deepest fear is that we are powerful beyond measure.
It is our light, not our darkness that frightens us.
We ask ourselves
Who am I to be so brilliant, gorgeous, talented, fabulous?
Actually
Who are we not to be?
You are a child of God ...
Your playing small doesn't serve the world.
There is nothing enlightened about shrinking so that other people won't feel insecure around you, we are all meant to shine, as children do, we are born to make manifest the glory of God, that is within us.
It is not just in some of us; it is in everyone.
And as we let our own light shine, we unconsciously give other people permission to do the same.
As we're liberated from our own fears, our presence automatically liberates others

A poem frequently attributed to Nelson Mandela, after he quoted it in his inauguration speech in 1993.

The Dead Good Funerals Book

PART ONE
TODAY'S FUNERAL INDUSTRY

The UK Funeral Market

In the UK the funeral market is currently estimated to be worth around £800 million annually with around 640,000 funerals taking place each year. There are an estimated 4,000 funeral directors at present offering services. Funeral directors are not subject to any licensing or control, nor are they required to have professional qualifications or be registered. Entry into the market is, in consequence, not difficult, but a steady decline in the death rate means the only scope for growth in the market is the provision of additional or higher value services. The majority of funeral directors, around 65 per cent, are independently owned. The Co-operative movement has the largest number of 'funeral homes', with a single brand name in the UK, although some co-operative societies operate autonomously. Dignity was formed when the US-owned Service Corporation International (SCI) got into financial difficulties. It is the only other sizeable company in the market, owning both funeral homes, crematoria and cemeteries and currently has a market-share of approximately 12 per cent. The annual survey of funeral costs in Britain showed in 2000 a burial cost on average £2,048 (up 25% in two years) and cremation cost £1,215 (up 12% in two years). There are great regional variations in cost. Burial in London and the South East is 50% more expensive than the North.

Researchers found that the price of an identical funeral varied by hundreds of pounds between different funeral directors in the same district, so it is worthwhile getting at least two quotations.

Without question, we end up having booked their cars and drivers and bearers, having bought the coffin from their predictably limited stock, having handed over the body of the deceased, probably to be embalmed, to be prepared for the coffin and dressed in the garments they have in stock. What if we don't like the style and design of any of the coffins or gowns in the catalogue? Who designed them? Who made the selection? How could we get anything different? We're pressed, through shortage of time, to make the best of it, yet why should we? As consumers, we are under no obligation to modify our wishes to meet the aspirations of traders in the field – and we have the Office of Fair Trading behind us all the way. Their concern is that information about options should be made available to members of the public and that nothing should stop people having such information if that is what they want.

> "He was marvellous – he took all the pressure off – all we had to do was pay the bill."

> "They bent over backwards to be kind. I relied completely on them."

> "I was asked all the time to decide on details immediately, whereas I feel this could have been left until the following day when I was not so upset."

Some decisions can wait till next day. Offers from the polished professional to "see to everything" prey upon our vulnerability and our reticence. We may be concerned about the price, yet in no way disrespectful in our attitude to the dead. Funeral Directors have subtle ways of expressing their expectations that we will want only the best for our elderly relative and these are hard to refute when we feel guilty of neglecting them a little. Even harder is asking straightforward questions about how much it is all going to cost, and what the extras will be. Oddfellows Survey of Funeral Costs in Britain 2000 quotes:

> "Over the last 10 years we have found that funeral directors have tended to "hide" the true cost of funerals. This means that the service is "sold" at a much lower price than the final amount the client actually pays. Most funerals are organised by a close family member, often at a time of great stress. To find that the bill has grown by 30% - 150% is not going to help."

The funeral industry has invented elaborate rituals and seeks to persuade us that these are 'traditional'. Preying on our vulnerability, our anxiety, our guilt even, it is not difficult to see how a funeral can become manipulated into being a display of status. The professionals have to focus on the bereaved, since they seldom knew the person who has died. The family and friends at this time focus on the person who has died. Here is potential conflict of interests and confusion around the focus of the funeral.

For example, there are two conflicting ways to read the image of a small bunch of wild flowers on the coffin, picked by a child. On the one hand it shows more about love and shared walks with a caring grandparent than any tonnage of cellophane hot-house bouquets from the professional florists. On the other hand, it appears they did not think much about grand-dad and were too mean to spend money on a decent show of flowers. It's hard to fight public taste and snobbery, especially at such a stressful time.

Debi, a friend, told how her father died a gentle peaceful death at home after scarcely any illness, and the family kept the body at the house, and decided to prepare him for burial in his favourite gardening clothes – the old shoes, his corduroys, the cardigan mended on the elbow. That was more him than any stiff, dark suit – but why is 'keeping it in the family' disapproved of? It's personal, it's truthful, it's caring, it's 'hands-on', but it turns over less money on the balance sheet of the funeral industry – it jars against our culture of constant economic growth.

The growth of professional services and escalating costs is directly related to spiritual and social impoverishment. We live in a system where every time money changes hands we count ourselves richer, no matter what damage may be inherent in the transaction. The problem of capitalism, as Dr Tony Walter so succinctly puts it in his book **Funerals and how to improve them**, is not that funerals cost too much, but that they cost at all.

Production line funerals are a prime example of this. At the end of the day, who are they for? A mother told us of her infant son's funeral, where she felt an outsider, not a participant. Many people we meet would like to see change. Some have faced a friend's funeral and not known what to do. Many have come out afterwards feeling the funeral did not represent what the person believed in life. We need a framework and resource material to hand, not strait-jackets.

Funerals as
a Victorian Invention

Today's funerals are a Victorian invention, or at least, poor vestiges of past style. The Victorians "invented" the coffin, the hearse, the black clothes, granite memorials, burial gowns, drapes and most of all the job of funeral director. We unquestioningly go on, the way we were brought up, to regard funerals as if that is the way they have to be. The only difference is that petrol is used instead of horsepower to pull the hearse.

Why is there a coffin? It is not required by law. Before 1750 everyone in Europe, except the aristocracy, was buried in a blanket off the bed. Wool first. Later linen was used. A shroud is a possible alternative today – see **Natural Burials**. If the grave had a marker, it used to be made out of wood. It is a fallacy to say wood will not last. Look at the doors on any ancient church.

Funeral directors have created the mystique that a funeral is an unfathomable and difficult thing that only they, as experts, know about. With the decline in church attendance, we turn less to the clergy and give authority to funeral directors instead. Their commercial basis means that in handing over to them the possibility of exploitation comes in.

In the relationship between the funeral director and the client, the former has a marked psychological and commercial advantage, so that the balance of bargaining power is tilted in his favour. This warning from the Office of Fair Trading (OFT) is backed up with statistics showing that, owing to the distress of the bereavement, those who seek the funeral director's services rarely obtain more than one estimate.

Because of their lack of knowledge and their distress, funeral arrangers are vulnerable and need a measure of protection. People do not arrange funerals often enough to acquire the background knowledge which guides them when they make other major purchases, and they may be in no state of mind to make best use of such knowledge as they have. The OFT believes that some form of intervention, directed in particular at making the service provided by funeral directors more accurately match the preference of funeral arrangers, is necessary and desirable. They caution the industry not to take too much comfort from the low complaints figures since, in this sensitive area, most people are too upset to complain about the standards of service or the price and want to put the whole affair behind them. For further information see **Resources and Contacts**.

Travel Agent/Funeral Agent

L et us, with respect, compare two industries: the travel industry and the funerals industry. We are, thankfully, more familiar with the former than the latter, although both are concerned with journeys, in their different ways.

Last minute holiday deals on teletext and bargain flights booked on-line do not suit everyone, hence the continued presence of travel agents on our high streets. We feel we can use the travel agent to supply us with what we want. We feel in control of the transaction, we specify when, where, how much? Some clients are independent travellers. Their requirements are basic but important: reservations on ships or aeroplanes, travel insurance and visa information. Apart from that, they prefer to make their own arrangements, not necessarily to save money, but to have the freedom to please themselves. This aspect of the work does not mean commercial ruin for the travel agent. It forms part of the service they offer, with adequate margins built in.

Many people prefer a package. They "buy" a holiday, and pay up in full in advance, before they get there, for their accommodation, all the meals they will consume, all their drinks from the bar (in some schemes), their cycle and windsurfing hire, their entertainment, their excursions, without much knowledge of what the place will be like or what is actually offered. Much more money passes through the hands of the travel agent before it is dispersed. But this option is not for everyone.

Returning to the comparison with the funerals industry, present practice is much closer to the latter example where a complete package is on offer. If it suits, that's fine. Excellent value with no worries, and no responsibilities for the client. What we hope is that the funerals industry will realise also that there are clients akin to the independent traveller. They need and want to buy certain services, but there are things they want to take responsibility for and make decisions about themselves. These clients are thoughtful and discerning and willing to put time in to do their own research thoroughly if their venture is to be successful and satisfying.

As far as commercial success is concerned, the travel industry flourishes through its policy of offering a professional service tailored to the needs of the client. The funerals industry need not fear loss of trade now that people are beginning to challenge their dominant role. The shrewd ones will continue to prosper by recognising this change and adapting their practice to become more flexible. Only those unwilling to adapt will find they have fewer clients.

Fears of a Pauper's Funeral

The Victorians' attitude to the shame of debt led them to create savings schemes designed to ensure that, if nothing else, the funeral could be paid for. There was no shame in poverty, but great shame in a pauper's funeral. This shame hides a fear, with a very real source. The body of anyone dying "on the parish", not provided for and without relatives to arrange a funeral, could be handed over for medical dissection. This was a terrifying 'punishment' for anyone not able to afford their own funeral.

In the 17th and 18th centuries, dismemberment and dissection were sentences for certain convicted criminals, more feared than capital punishment. In 1832 it stopped being legal to cut up criminals, so that the poor and destitute were denied a funeral and substituted as an alternative for the surgeons to practise on.

In Brazil today, where the cities include millions existing in poverty (some making their shanty dwellings in old tombs in historic graveyards), the need to ensure for themselves a proper funeral with a coffin and a single grave is very strong, particularly among people who have never owned anything in life.

Through grandmothers and great grandmothers and the cultural values of the poor they inherited and passed on to their thrifty daughters, we still have close links with this fear. On the moorlands above Leek in Staffordshire stands Flash, proud to be the highest village in England. Each summer, "The Tea Pot Club" holds the "Tea Pot Feast" and a procession through the village with their banner. For generations the Club has been a way of putting small amounts of money away regularly, towards funeral costs. Changes in legislation obliged the Tea Pot Club to be wound up in 1995, with a special ceremony for the last procession (should it have been a symbolic funeral – perhaps the burial of a teapot?).

Survey of Funeral Costs in Britain

Burials

	Average quote	Average actual price	Cost difference	Real price over quote
London	£1,131	£2,646	£1,515	**134%**
North	£892	£1,741	£849	**95%**
South East	£868	£1,835	£967	**111%**

Cremations

	Average quote	Average actual price	Cost difference	Real price over quote
London	£980	£1,362	£382	**39%**
North	£956	£1,382	£426	**44%**
South East	£894	£1,835	£967	**108%**

Source of information in tables: Oddfellows Survey of Funeral Costs in Britain 2000

Funeral Industry Products

Before we are invited to go and pay our last respects to our nearest and dearest in the Chapel of Rest, they have been groomed and prepared by someone who has never seen them alive. These practitioners use a series of technical products including plastic chin rests, mouth formers, "natural expression" formers, cosmetic thread, cosmetic creams (in a range of colours from light flesh to mulberry), eye caps (plain or perforated) and restorative wax. This is doubtless a skilled profession, but it can turn someone familiar to us into a complete stranger after death.

Products for "after coffining" include:

- the Inflatable Pillow which deflates silently when the coffin is closed and

- Mortuary Gowns which come in standard male and female, luxury male and female (satin finish front). What is offensive is the simulation of night clothes to assist the illusion of sleep so appropriate for the Chapel of Rest.

It is too easy to flip through the product catalogues and make statements that are cynical and critical. The catalogues also reveal the other truly honourable side of the work: transportation of bodies, the post-mortem, post-accident, post-exhumation, post-emergency and disaster work that goes on, with all the necessary products for personal safety of paramedic and rescue services. This is work that few of us would be willing to deal with.

Embalming

The Green Movement is actively looking at many aspects of funerals: land use; set aside; woodland management schemes; investigation into pollution and environmental damage from the use of harmful materials (eg chipboard coffins, toxic glues and plastic veneers for burial and/or cremation). Embalming itself as a process deserves a watchdog.

When the discreet question is posed as to whether we might wish to visit the deceased to say good-bye, the implications can be regrettable in more ways than one. Apart from the cost of an extra service being added to the bill, we may not be satisfied with the results (see **Funeral Industry Products**) but mainly on environmental grounds embalming is extremely bad news.

It is plainly not necessary (except for an extended lying in state). Eight pints of blood are removed. Where do they go?

There is no legislation covering this, so presumably they go down the drains. Strange at a time when consciousness about blood is so acute. Then, eight pints of embalming fluid are pumped into the body. This embalming fluid is imported from the USA – another example of unnecessary international transportation.

The embalmed body is about to be buried or cremated. Do we want to be putting that quantity of chemicals into the earth? Or into the atmosphere? Why do we do it? We can only imagine it is not in the interests of the funeral director to sit down with us and go through the implications, to enable us to make an informed decision.

Freelance embalmers, who need not be licensed, are on call in all parts of the country.

The addition of embalming fluid to body tissue brings about a chemical reaction which forms an inert and chemically different substance. The most widely-used preservative chemical in embalming fluids is formaldehyde (also present in some plants), which is a toxic substance. However, the amount in concentrated arterial injection fluid varies from about 18% to 30% by volume, the most widely-purchased chemical being 26% by volume.

This is used in a diluted form of about 1.6% formaldehyde by volume, for injection into the circulatory system. As 80% of the human body is water, therefore a further dilution of the formaldehyde takes place following injection; it then combines with the cell protoplasm to form the inert substances referred to. At these high levels of dilution, any degree of toxicity remaining would be at an extremely low level, and would indeed be lower than substances produced in the normal body. A concentrated cavity fluid is injected into the hollow organs with a higher level of formaldehyde concentration. This is quickly absorbed into the tissues, effecting the chemical changes previously referred to.

by Peter J. Ball, FBIE, National General Secretary, BIE writing in Funeral Services Journal, November 1994

DEFYING GRAVITY
Roger McGough

Gravity is one of the oldest tricks in the book.
Let go of the book and it abseils to the ground
As if, at the centre of the earth, spins a giant yo-yo
To which everything is attached by an invisible string.

Tear out a page of the book and make an aeroplane.
Launch it.   For an instant it seems that you have fashioned
A shape that can outwit air, that has slipped the knot.
But no.   The earth turns, the winch tightens, it is wound in.

One of my closest friends is, at the time of writing,
Attempting to defy gravity, and will surely succeed.
Eighteen months ago he was playing rugby,
Now, seven stones lighter, his wife carries him aw-

Kwardly from room to room.   Arranges him gently
Upon the sofa for the visitors.   'How are things?'
Asks one, not wanting to know.   Pause.   'Not too bad.'
(Open brackets. Condition inoperable.   Close brackets.)

Soon now, the man that I love (not the armful of bones)
Will defy gravity.   Freeing himself from the tackle
He will sidestep the opposition and streak down the wing
Towards a dimension as yet unimagined.

Back where the strings are attached there will be a service
And homage paid to the giant
yo-yo.   A box of left-overs
Will be lowered into a space on
loan from the clay.
Then, weighted down, the
living will walk wearily away.

PART TWO
WHAT TO DO WHEN
SOMEBODY DIES

Information taken from the original draft of the Charter for the Bereaved written by Ken West

So it is time to set out some information about what a funeral consists of, how it is arranged and in what sequence. We all have a right to know this information, as a basis on which to make informed choices. The value of this knowledge is that it enables us to bring about change, where we feel it is necessary, or at least to make better and wiser decisions. To achieve this, we are pleased to use information from the original 1995 draft of the Charter for the Bereaved, developed for the Institute of Cemetery and Crematorium Management (ICCM), and written by Ken West whilst employed as Bereavement Services Manager at Carlisle. He is currently manager at Croydon. (See **Resources and Contacts** if you require a copy of the Charter)

What to do when Somebody Dies begins with a section which describes what occurs prior to the funeral. Everyone should read that. It is followed by a clear step by step account of what to do when organising a burial and the more complex procedure of organising a cremation. About 71% of people now choose cremation. The sections conclude with information on different types of graves and memorials.

The period prior to a Funeral

Death at Home

When a person dies at home, the next of kin or executor and the family doctor should be informed. The doctor who cared for the person during the last illness will complete a free Certificate of the Cause of Death (called the "death certificate" hereafter). If cremation is intended, this doctor will complete cremation Form B and will arrange for another doctor to complete the confirmatory Form C. The second doctor will need to view the body at some stage. These forms are provided free of charge from the crematorium. The two doctors will require payment for completing the forms (approximately £45.00 per form in 2003). These forms are not required if the death is reported to the Coroner.

The death certificate must be taken to the Registrar of Births and Deaths in the sub-district where the death occurred, within five days. In Scotland, you can visit any Registrar of Births and Deaths. The doctor, funeral director (if used) or Citizens' Advice Bureau will give you the address. Ensure you visit the correct office and check opening times, as they may operate limited hours. The doctor may send the death certificate direct to the Registrar, and not give it to you to take. Regardless, the next of kin or whoever is arranging the funeral will have to visit the Registrar and give information about the death.

Death in Hospital

If someone dies in hospital, the death certificate will be completed automatically by a doctor. The next of kin may need to authorise a post-mortem, if the hospital need to confirm the cause of death before the death certificate is issued. If cremation is intended, the hospital should be told and they will arrange the completion of the cremation forms B and C. On some occasions, the hospital may avoid the need to complete Form C, which will save you the cost of this certificate.

The body will be transferred to the mortuary as soon as possible. Arrangements to get the death certificate to the Registrar of Births and Deaths, and register the death are as above, under **Death at Home**. The Registrar will be the one that covers the Hospital area, which may be different from the home address of the deceased.

If the death occurs in a residential or nursing home, they may follow a similar routine. In addition, they may have an arrangement with a Funeral Director for the removal of the body to the mortuary or Chapel of Rest. This funeral director does not have to undertake the funeral for you, neither should they canvass your business. You can choose your own funeral director, or direct the funeral without one, as you so wish.

Coroner

If the death was sudden or due to an accident, or no doctor had attended for some time, then the Coroner must be informed. The Registrar of Births and Deaths may also report the death to the Coroner, if the cause of death is unclear, or may not be due to natural causes. The Coroner will decide whether to hold a post-mortem, and/or an inquest. Most cases are found to be due to natural causes and as an inquest will not be required, the Coroner will notify the Registrar that the death can be registered. The next of kin will need to visit the Registrar to do this. The Coroner's Officer will keep the next of kin informed about what to do. As these arrangements will cause delay, you must not arrange the funeral until authorised by the Coroner's Officer. The Coroner will issue an Order for Burial (white) or for Cremation (yellow). The certificate should be given to your funeral director or sent to the cemetery or crematorium as soon as possible.

The collection of the body after an accident, or for a post-mortem ordered by the Coroner, will be contracted out to a funeral director. This funeral director does not have to direct the funeral for you.

Registrar of Births and Deaths

The Registrar of Births and Deaths can only register the death if he/she is given or has obtained the death certificate or has received notification from the Coroner. He or she will require to know the following details about the deceased:

1   Full name – including any other names they were known by.

2   Maiden surname – if the deceased is a married woman.

3   Date and Place of Birth.

4   Occupation – and their husband's full name and occupation, if the deceased is a married woman or a widow.

You will need to confirm the date and place of death. Other questions will be asked about date of birth of the surviving spouse, and information about state pensions and allowances that the person was receiving, including war pensions. The

Funeral Directors' Services

Funeral Directors will manage funeral arrangements and give advice and support to the bereaved. There is a code of practice that requires funeral directors to provide full information about their services and prices. The price list should include the cost of a basic funeral.

A basic funeral includes the services of the funeral director who will:

– make all the necessary arrangements

– provide appropriate staff

– provide a suitable coffin

– transfer the deceased from the place of death to the funeral parlour, during normal working hours (up to 10 miles)

– care for the deceased prior to the funeral

– provide a hearse to the nearest cemetery or crematorium

– arrange for a burial or cremation

A basic funeral does not include:

– embalming

– viewing of the deceased

– providing transport for the bereaved

– paying fees on behalf of the bereaved

Other fees, often called 'disbursements', will be payable to cover the charges of the cemetery or crematorium. Ask the funeral director for an accurate quotation detailing all these fees.

Funeral Payments – these are funds intended to help you towards the cost of the funeral if you are on a low income. They are recoverable from the deceased's estate, contact your local Social Security Office for further information.

If you have a complaint regarding the service you receive, you should firstly contact the funeral director in question. If you are not satisfied with the response you can contact:

Local Consumer Advisory Service

The Funeral Standards Council - 02920 38 2046

The National Association of Funeral Directors – 0121 711 1343

The Natural Death Centre gives free advice on organising a funeral without a funeral director.

NHS number will be requested and the medical card of the deceased should be surrendered to the Registrar, if it is available. If the number is not known, and the medical card is unavailable, you can still register the death.

The Registrar will issue a free social security form to ensure that benefits are being paid correctly. If the Coroner is not issuing an Order for Burial or Cremation, the Registrar will issue a certificate (green) for this purpose. This should be given to your funeral director or sent to the cemetery or crematorium as soon as possible. The Registrar will advise you over any further certificate copies you require. These will be for obtaining grant of probate or letters of administration, to show banks, social security or building societies, and to claim insurances.

Caring for the body

While the above procedures are taking place, it is essential that the body is cared for. With death at home, if you are using a funeral director, he or she should be called as soon as possible. They will remove the body and complete laying-out and possibly embalming. The body may stay at their Chapel of Rest or may be returned home, should you so wish. If the death was in hospital, the staff will lay out the body of the deceased. Your funeral director will collect the body, and carry out your instructions.

If you are not using a funeral director, and the death occurs at home, you must complete laying out yourself, or have this done by a district nurse or some other person. The body can be kept at home and must be kept as cool as possible. Your local mortuary, cemetery or crematorium may have facilities to hold the body pending the funeral.

If the death was in hospital, the body will be laid out and taken to the hospital mortuary. You can collect the body yourself, provided you have a coffin and transport, and keep it at home, or you may be able to retain the body at the mortuary until the day of the funeral.

Conclusion

It is assumed that whoever arranges the funeral is aware of the wishes of the deceased, whether a will exists and who the executor(s) are. It is important to note that executors have the right to choose burial or cremation, whether it accords with the wishes of the deceased or not. If there is no will, and therefore no executors, the next of kin should make these decisions. With a greater number of people taking out funeral plans and insurances, it is important to check whether the deceased subscribed to a scheme or policy.

Death Abroad

If the person has died in Scotland or abroad and it is intended to bury or cremate the body in England or Wales, it is necessary to obtain:

■ A death certificate issued by the civil registrar of the place where the death occurred, with a translation where necessary or

■ An authorisation to remove the body, or in Scotland, a copy of a certified extract from the entry in the Scottish death register or a letter from the Procurator Fiscal stating place and cause of death.

These must be produced to the Registrar of Births and Deaths for the district where the funeral is to take place, in order that a Certificate of No Liability to Register the death can be issued. This Certificate, together with the forms from abroad or Scotland must be passed to the cemetery or crematorium as soon as possible.

Burial Procedure

Provisional Booking

As soon as the death has been certified, and the availability of the minister (if needed) is confirmed, the cemetery is telephoned and a provisional funeral booking is arranged. (The cemetery office should be available for booking during normal office hours, and perhaps over weekends). The following information will be required:

■ Cemetery location – the office may control a number of cemeteries and the precise one should be identified.

■ Funeral date and time – this will be when the funeral arrives at the cemetery gates, or at the cemetery chapel, if this is used. A suitably dressed cemetery employee should meet and guide the funeral during the period in the cemetery. At no time should you be controlled by employees dressed in overalls, donkey jackets, etc. Normally, a minimum two days' notice is required, although sufficient time must be available to register the death and obtain all certificates.

- Name and address of the deceased.

- Grave number – if you already own the Rights to a grave, the number will be shown on the grave Deed. Sufficient space for a full burial must be available. If you do not have a grave, you need to specify a new grave, define the type and/or visit the cemetery to select one, if this is possible. The choice of grave is often very limited. If you are concerned about the precise position you should make a visit and arrange to be shown the available unused graves.

- The name and telephone number of the funeral director or the person arranging the funeral, who will also pay the required fees. A table of fees is available upon request.

The details above are the minimum necessary for a provisional booking. These will be sufficient to enable cemetery staff to locate an existing grave or allocate a new one, and to prepare for the excavation. If a memorial is placed upon an existing grave, arrangements to move it to allow the excavation will be urgently required. Most modern memorials are small headstone types, which can remain in position.

The details below can be given by telephone at this early stage, or sometime later, or entered on a "Notice of Burial":

- Coffin or container size – this is the overall size, including handles.

- Funeral type – this will depend upon how the funeral is organised. If a service is held prior to arrival at the cemetery, you may go "straight to grave" when you arrive. The grave will be dressed with grass mats, and a "committal" service or any other ceremony you may prefer, can take place at the graveside. Bearers will be necessary to carry the coffin from the vehicle to the grave, and to lower the coffin. Some cemeteries may provide bearers for a fee. If a cemetery chapel is available, for which a fee is usually payable, you can hold a service there first, and then follow the committal procedure outlined above.

- Religion of deceased – this is to enable the cemetery staff to anticipate the style and length of service, and to ensure that the correct plot is used, if denominational areas are available. At Church of England and Free Church funerals, some dry soil will be made available to sprinkle upon the coffin at the committal stage.

Notice of Burial

A formal notification of the burial must be delivered to the cemetery authority as soon as possible. A regulation allowing a minimum 24-hour notice is often specified. This form is issued free of charge, by post if requested. The completed form is a binding contract over the work and costs involved, which may be payable even if the funeral is cancelled or transferred to another cemetery.

The Notice of Burial should be accompanied by a Coroner's Order for Burial or a Registrar's Certificate. Although some authorities may accept the Order or Certificate when the funeral arrives, others will not and this has resulted in the funeral being delayed or cancelled. Alternative arrangements apply when the death occurred abroad, and the body is being brought in for burial.

Memorials

Decisions over a memorial should be taken during the period of reflective adjustment following the funeral. There is no rush. Some funeral directors sell memorials at the time of the funeral, and advice may be biased towards recommending a certain grave type, which may have future commercial advantage in the supplying of a memorial.

Whenever you do it, think about design and materials. A memorial mason is independent of the funeral director and can offer specialist as well as artistic advice. Check details of what the cemetery will accept by way of size and design before ordering or making a memorial.

Behind the Scenes

When the provisional booking is made, the registers are checked to locate the correct grave and a site visit may be carried out to check the memorial on the grave. If a new grave is required, one will be allocated. As soon as confirmation is received, an order to excavate the grave will be issued, which may involve using a contractor. A grave for two burials will be excavated and shored to a depth of 6' 0" (1.8m), which will leave 4' 6" (1.35m) depth for the burial of the second coffin on top of the first. The grave is excavated, then covered by boards, and may need regular checks in case of collapse and/ or water build-up

Prior to the funeral, the grave will have planks and boards placed around the edge, to support bearers and mourners, and will be dressed with artificial grass mats. These should be in good condition and should cover all the soil removed from the grave. Cemetery staff will guide the funeral to the correct grave, and will direct the bearers. They must place the coffin, with the head at the correct end, on two wooden spars placed adjacent to two or three tapes or webbing, across the grave. With the coffin resting on the two spars, often called putlogs, the tapes or webbing are folded around the coffin, often through the handles, with an end being taken by each of four or six bearers. At a given signal, they lift the coffin, the cemetery staff remove the putlogs, and the coffin is lowered slowly into the grave. The bearers then stand back and the service is completed. The cortège will leave the cemetery, as soon as they are ready. Most cemeteries allow access by vehicle, although where roads are restricted in size, or lead into cul-de-sacs, or are steep, pedestrian access may be enforced.

The method of using putlogs and lowering the coffin varies in different parts of the country, and this aspect should be confirmed.

The cemetery staff will stay at the graveside until all the family have left the site. The grave back-filling staff, who should be available in case of collapse, will stay out of sight until called forward. They will back-fill the grave, leaving the site neat and tidy, with the wreaths and flowers carefully placed. It is essential that the backfilled soil is compacted every six inches in depth by treading, to reduce the need for excessive re-instatements. Nonetheless, the grave soil will sink as compaction occurs, and particularly after heavy rainfall. This should be made up regularly, as a sunken grave upsets the bereaved relatives. The grave should be re-instated after some weeks or months, preferably by turfing or if this is not possible, by grass seeding the area. If a memorial was removed for the burial, this will be inscribed by a mason, providing one is instructed by the bereaved or executor, and re-fixed as soon as the backfilled soil is sufficiently settled.

The cemetery office will maintain contact with the funeral

director or person arranging the funeral, whilst the grave excavation is ongoing. This accommodates changes to the funeral arrangements, where these are necessary. They will routinely issue receipts for the payment of the Right of Burial in the grave and/or the burial fee (NB payment to ministers and organists is made direct to the person concerned.)

After the burial, the legal requirements will be completed. The Registrar or staff will enter the burial in the Register of Burials, and in the index to these records. An entry for a new grave will be made in the Register of Graves, recording the purchase of the Right of Burial and the period that this covers. A Grant of Right of Burial will be prepared and posted to the grave purchaser within a specified period. New graves will be marked off the cemetery grave plans. Since 1986, when legal approval was given, many authorities now maintain burial records on computer. These records must be maintained forever and are available for enquiries and research. You have a right, as next of kin or executor, to inspect cemetery records where you suspect they are incorrect or contain erroneous information.

Within 96 hours of the burial, the detachable portion of the Coroner's or Registrar's Certificate must be sent to the Registrar indicating the date and place of burial. It is important to note that the place of burial is not actually recorded by the Registrar, and subsequently locating the place of burial through the Registration Service is not possible.

The cemetery office remains the focal point for any further concern with the grave or burial. Many of the contacts will be associated with any memorial placed on the grave. After the first burial in the grave, the widow or widower may order a memorial. The mason involved will send the application to erect this to the cemetery office. The application will be checked to ensure the memorial design accords with any regulations, and the precise names and dates in the inscription will be checked against the burial record. If approved and upon payment of a fee, the mason will be given permission to place the memorial. The design and erection of the memorial must be safe, and the construction and correct location will be verified by a member of the cemetery staff. Subsequently, the mason will apply to place additional inscriptions upon the memorial, subject to payment of a fee, as further burials take place.

Avoiding errors

It is extremely important to ensure that the burial occurs in the correct grave. It is easy to forget that a busy cemetery may be receiving many burials each day.

This is generally avoided by a requirement for a staff member at the central office being appointed to check the excavation of every grave, and subsequently to attend the burial service, checking the coffin plate before burial. Where this does not occur, and these instructions are given by post, telephone or fax, particularly when the on-site work is done by contractors, the cemetery authority should be able to demonstrate that they are ensuring the correct coffin is placed in the correct grave. Although it is expensive to complete these checks, the work involved is covered by the fees paid and is a necessary part of the service.

Development of Cemeteries

In the past, cemeteries offered a wide choice of grave types, with an associated variety of memorials. Due to various reasons, such cemeteries fell into disrepair. Consequently, the choice of grave became limited and gradually, a perception developed that memorials were a nuisance and that they should be rigidly controlled as to size and design. Added to this was a concentration on grounds' maintenance costs. The culmination of these two aspects was the introduction of the lawn-type grave.

The lawn type grave is generally the only option available at most cemeteries where it is seen as the cheapest maintenance regime, allowing unimpeded yet intensive mowing along the lawns between parallel rows of identical headstones. The loss of individuality, artistic skill and any element of choice is evident. The absence of full-grave memorials and/or kerb surrounds allows people to walk unimpeded over the lawn grave. This upsets some and is specifically prohibited by some religions.

This restriction on burial choice has occurred in parallel with the increasing adoption of cremation. Consequently, in 2003, in 71% of cases cremation was chosen. The excessive promotion of cremation has been recognised by some and there is increasing emphasis on improving burial options in some areas. This has concentrated on offering a wider choice of graves, including a "green" or natural form of burial, and generally to widen memorial choice.

The natural burial option is available as woodland burial in some parts of the country. This involves burial followed by the planting of a tree. Subsequently, the "return to nature" concept allows the graves to form a nature reserve, without routine maintenance or the use of chemicals. The natural burial ground offers environmental benefits including habitat for wildlife and in the long term may form part of a community woodland or country park. Restrictions on the use of embalming and a requirement to use biodegradable coffins might apply. Schemes and costs do vary, particularly if you are not resident in the vicinity. Some private, farm-based schemes are now developing and variations on natural burial are arising, eg wildflower meadow burials.

Most graves are "bought", thereby reserving them for the burial of specific persons. The reference to buying a grave is not strictly correct. The "Right of Burial" is purchased, giving the owner control over the burials in the grave, and the

Bereaved Parents

It is traditional to inter babies in a white coffin which is normally made from chipboard covered by a white cloth. Some parents feel that a coffin is too harsh and hard a container for a child and prefer to use woollen shrouds, wicker or "Moses" baskets and other "softer" containers. Should they so wish, this can allow the parent or parents personally to place the child in what they feel is a more "comfortable" position. Increasing the personal input of the parents benefits the parent psychologically and helps in their subsequent grieving. Placing photographs or other personal items with the body or carrying the coffin or container are examples of this.

Many parents appear to benefit from the location of baby graves in specific sections. This prevents them from feeling that they are isolated and alone with their loss. They can see, and meet, other parents and experience the deaths of other babies through existing memorials and inscriptions. It is very important that the babies' graves are not seen to "fill-in" narrow verge edges, or pieces of land unsuitable for adult burial.

right to place a memorial. The ground, itself, is still in the ownership of the landowner. The right cannot be purchased for a period in excess of 100 years, and much shorter periods are usually offered. You can reserve the right in advance, if you wish to secure a grave in a certain area, or if you wish to save the cost when you die. Most graves allow for two burials, one above the other. As each burial takes place, you will be charged an additional interment fee.

You have the right to be buried in an unpurchased "common" grave. In the past, unpurchased graves were used for many burials. These graves are still available and as no Right of Burial is given, are inexpensive. They are used for unrelated burials, and no right to place a memorial, or indeed, to place a vase or flowers upon the grave, is given. They were also known as "paupers' graves". (Also see **Churchyard Reuse**)

Baby and Infant Graves

As a consequence of medical and social improvements, a stillbirth or baby death is a rare experience in modern times. In view of the smaller numbers, the bereaved parents can

Recommendations

The arrangements between the hospital and the cemetery vary considerably throughout the country but should allow for certain basic requirements. As an example any scheme should allow for individual burial, in individual small graves. The grave should either be given into the ownership of the family for an agreed term, or ownership should remain with the cemetery, and the grave given free of charge to the family, without any formal agreement. Any suggestion that this represents a common or pauper grave must be avoided. The bereaved should be able to place a memorial, vases and tributes, as they would on a private grave, and there should be no restrictions. In fact, where successful schemes are operating, it is noticeable that the parents or family need to place teddy bears, dolls and other baby-related items on the grave. This should be accommodated by the grave design (by a hard surface at the head of the grave) and not regulated against. The memorial regulations should allow baby-related designs, ie teddy bears, angels, hearts, etc. and accommodate inscriptions of a colloquial and familiar nature.

feel isolated and need good advice and support. As part of this, it is essential that the funeral satisfies their needs. The development of more sensitive options is needed to ensure that parents can grieve properly.

Baby funerals generally fall into two categories. Firstly, where the funeral is arranged through a hospital and secondly, where it is privately arranged by the family. This item considers burial facilities in cemeteries and you should refer to **Cremation Procedure** for that choice of funeral.

1   Hospital arrangements – this usually involves an agreement with a "contract" funeral director and a specific cemetery. A special area may be designated at the cemetery for these burials, perhaps called the "Babies' Memorial Garden" or similar. The burial, typically using a small white coffin,

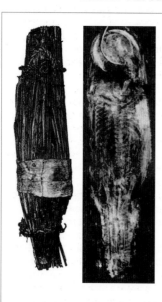

Archaeological Digs have revealed two interesting ancient practices, that could be a source of inspiration. On Birkrigg Common, South Cumbria, a baby who had died had been buried in a swan's wing – a gentle, loving and caring image resonating with a mysterious poetry all its own. Enveloping wings, protecting, soft and warming, yet strong and powerful. Flight, the journey ...

A radiographic survey of a small reed coffin showed the skeleton of a baby inside a bundle of reeds. Reminiscent of a sheaf of corn on the outside, yet in the craft of making it to fulfil its purpose, it is bound round towards either end, enclosing the baby, swaddled like a papoose, and protecting its frailty. So it becomes both coffin and cradle at the same time. Lined with moss or leaves we imagine something the mother could still hold in her arms before saying good-bye. Journey imagery is so strong here – the infant Moses in the bulrushes, a precious cargo carried to safety.

The Dead Good Funerals Book

will take place at an agreed time, to which the family will be invited. The grave will be dressed with artificial grass mats and a service will take place, if desired by the family. It is important that such funerals are treated individually and are not subjected to a lesser quality than that offered for "private" funerals.

The hospital service is offered for stillbirth (a baby born dead after the 24th week of pregnancy) and babies born alive, who subsequently die. It is assumed that in the case of a home delivery, this service would also be available. More recently, in some areas, this burial option has been offered in cases of foetal loss, from 16 to 24 weeks of pregnancy. This is to prevent such bodies being placed in the hospital incinerator.

The hospital authorities generally do not charge for these burial arrangements. They also pay any necessary cemetery fees, although many public authorities offer their cemetery services free of charge in these cases. It is your right to be offered an infant grave. Your right and period of grave ownership will be defined, and you will be able to place a memorial in accordance with the regulations in force.

2   Private arrangements will be made if the hospital option is not available or is otherwise unsatisfactory. Also, if the parent(s) dislike the cemetery or graves used, they may prefer to make their own arrangements. When making private arrangements you may have the option to choose the scheme outlined above or you may prefer to buy a "private" grave.

It is important that the parents consider their own death and funeral at this time. This is because many cemeteries will allow the parents to purchase a full-size grave for an infant burial, with the burial(s) of the parent(s) taking place above the infant many years later. This opportunity for the parents and infant to be together may be greatly appreciated. It is an important consideration and the decision must be made quickly, before the funeral details are finalised. This will require the excavation of the grave to a greater depth and size, which may entail higher costs.

Farm and Garden Burials

The advantages of this form of burial allow you to organise a very personal funeral, in which you maintain total control. You are able to reduce costs significantly by avoiding the use of a funeral director, by making your own coffin or dispensing with this altogether, and not having to purchase a grave in a cemetery. It is important that you obtain permission to complete a burial, where you are not the landowner of the ground involved.

Farmland locations are rarely overlooked and will not offend neighbours or the public at large. The grave site should be on dry land and should be sufficient distance from watercourses, not to pose a pollution threat. In general avoid being within 50 metres of any well or borehole. Keep 10 metres from any standing or running water. Electrical or other services must obviously be avoided. A single burial, perhaps two burials, over a period of time will not constitute a "change of use" and no planning approval is thereby necessary. Exceeding this number of burials would require approval as a cemetery rather than as a farm!

Two major concerns influence the choice of a garden as a burial site. Firstly, the burial could be exhumed by any new property purchaser, and re-buried in a cemetery. This reason for obtaining an exhumation licence has yet to be tested, but would seem feasible. There are legal means (restrictive covenant) by which you can ensure the grave remains untouched, but this will involve costs and other uncertainties.

Secondly, the burial will not be registered. In effect, neither the name and personal details nor the grave location will be maintained in an official sense. This, of course, is unlike burials in the cemeteries which are recorded in perpetuity. In later times, nobody can locate the grave or find the burial details from an official source. If the grave is disturbed by building or excavation works at some stage in the future, the finding of the body will be reported to the police.

A certificate for burial issued by a coroner or Registrar of Births and Deaths will have to be obtained. The detachable section of this is completed and returned after the burial. Depending upon the circumstances, you may find it difficult to obtain a funeral director to help you with this type of burial. You can of course do the funeral without a funeral director.

Burial at Sea

Whilst an appealing option, in practice burial at sea is quite a complex procedure, with lengthy guidelines from the authorities. There are concerns regarding bodies being washed up on shore or disturbed near busy shipping and fishing areas. Currently there are three places off the English coast where sea burial is permitted:

- The Needles Spoil Ground, to the west of the Isle of Wight

- Nine miles from the mouth of the river Tyne

- A site near Newhaven

Contact your local fisheries District Inspector for more information

Further details of method are also given in the Natural Death Handbook (see **Resources & Contacts**)

An alternative to burial at sea is to dispose of your ashes at sea. This is possible almost anywhere. **green fuse** (see **Resources & Contacts**) sell beautiful urns made of compressed salt and sand which dissolve on the sea bed in less than an hour.

Cremation Procedures

Preliminary Application

As soon as the death has been certified, and the availability of the minister (if needed) is confirmed, the crematorium is telephoned and a provisional funeral booking is arranged. The following information will be required:

■ Funeral date and time – this will be when the funeral arrives at the crematorium chapel, where you will be met by a member of staff. Normally, a minimum three days' notice will be given, but this is dependent on the time needed to obtain the cremation medical certificates and the Registrar's Certificate or Coroner's Order. Services may be booked at fixed times, and dependent upon the crematorium, may range from 20 to 45 minutes apart. It may be possible to book extra time if it is needed.

■ Name and address of the deceased.

■ The name and telephone number of the funeral director,

or the person arranging the funeral, who will also pay the required fees. A table of fees is available upon request.

■ The details are the minimum necessary for a provisional booking. This enables the funeral director or person arranging the funeral to notify everybody involved, and ensure that they work within the time-scales.

The arrangements which follow involve far more forms and bureaucracy than applies to burial. This is because cremation destroys the body and, unlike burial, it cannot subsequently be recovered for investigation if crime or some other problem arises. The procedure appears complex, but is easily followed with the guidance of crematoria staff. All the forms are provided free of charge, and are now described:

1 Notice of Cremation: This form gives notice of the cremation and forms a binding contract regarding the payment of fees to the cremation authority. The following details will be required:

☐ The full name and address of the deceased, age and occupation.

☐ Whether a coffin or casket is being used.

☐ Service date and time. A time must be booked, even when a service is not being held. This is because every coffin is received formally through the chapel, without exception. A coffin cannot be accepted through the "back door".

☐ Service details, including minister's name, if attending, religion and music or other requests.

☐ Details on the placement of cremated remains. The applicant for cremation must indicate what is to happen to these and sign the form.

Other miscellaneous items may be requested on this form, including a choice of container for the cremated remains and whether the Chapel of Rest is to be used (see below for details). Some authorities offer bearers or other facilities at extra cost, and these need to be indicated. If the cremated remains are being buried in a churchyard, cemetery or some other crematorium, a Cremation Certificate can be requested. A small fee may apply, and the certificate is evidence that the cremation was completed by that Cremation Authority.

2   Form "A" – Application for Cremation: this is a statutory form issued under the Cremation Acts. It must be completed by the nearest surviving relative or executor. If not, a reason why some other person has applied must be given. The details required are quite straightforward, although the applicant must state that they have no reason to suppose the death was due to violence, poison, privation or neglect. A householder known to the applicant must countersign the form.

3   Medical Forms B, C, & F: these are statutory forms, subject to direct payment upon completion to the doctor involved. Form B is completed by the doctor who attended the deceased before death, and Form C by a doctor who confirms the cause of death. The issue of these forms is outlined in the item **What to do when Somebody Dies**. The Form C is not required with some hospital deaths where a post-mortem has been completed. This only applies if the doctor who completes Form B is aware of the results of the post-mortem. Where this applies, the deceased's relatives do not have to pay for Form C.

Form F is completed by a doctor appointed as the Medical Referee to the Cremation Authority. He or she will sign the form, if satisfied that the statutory requirements are complied with, the cause of death definitely ascertained and there exists no reason for further enquiry or examination. The cremation will only take place after this form has been signed.

The above forms must be submitted to the crematorium office, usually early on the day preceding the day of cremation. They must be accompanied by the green certificate issued by the Registrar, as outlined in the item **What to do when Somebody Dies**. The above forms are required when the death is not reported to the coroner.

If the death is reported to the coroner (or Procurator Fiscal, in Scotland) then the above procedure is changed. Following a post-mortem and in some cases an inquest, a yellow Form E will be issued. This replaces both Forms B and C above, and the green Registrar's certificate. This form is free, which benefits the bereaved as it saves the cost of doctors' fees for Forms B and C.

The above procedure applies to all deaths, including a baby that might die a short time after birth. The procedure is altered slightly for the cremation of a stillborn child, and it should be noted that foetal remains can also be cremated. The details above describe the forms involved. The procedure in the office and then at the crematorium is now described.

Office Procedure

Following the booking of the cremation time, the cremation forms arrive at the office, either together or individually. These are collated, checked for error or unanswered questions, and if complete, inspected and signed by the Medical Referee. This enables an identity card to be issued for each cremation, and these, together with a list of daily service details, are passed to the crematorium staff early each morning. After the cremation, the details about the deceased, the applicant for cremation and the doctors involved, are entered under a sequential number in a Register of Cremations (Form G), which is retained forever. An alphabetical index of those cremated is maintained, to facilitate searches in the future. This occurs often as time passes, mainly to identify the position of the cremated remains, particularly when those of a partner are to be placed in the same location.

Following a cremation, the cremated remains are placed according to the directions of the "applicant for cremation". This is the person who applies for, and signs the cremation Form "A". The signature or approval by letter, of this person, will be required whenever any changes of instruction take place.

It is a matter of choice whether the cremated remains are taken away or are left at the crematorium; these two options being considered below. The final location, of course, is closely associated with any form of memorialisation that is required, which is why these subjects are considered together.

Finally, and within 96 hours of the cremation, the detachable portion of the Coroner's or Registrar's Certificate will be sent to the Registrar, indicating the date and place of cremation.

Crematorium Procedures

The crematorium staff will place a list of all cremations that day, outside the crematorium chapel. The Supervisor and/ or chapel attendant will then meet each funeral and ensure that services run smoothly. This involves close liaison with ministers, organists and funeral directors. Where families are conducting funerals without a funeral director, the staff will advise and help.

If a Chapel of Rest is available, where coffins can be kept between death and the service, crematoria staff will help move the coffin to the chapel, at the agreed start time. Staff may also act as bearers, using a wheeled bier or physically carrying the coffin, and placing it on the catafalque, where it rests during the service. The staff will also control car parking, and may monitor activities using camera surveillance. The wreaths brought on coffins will be placed on the "flower terrace" or equivalent, and should be identified by a card or sign indicating the name of the deceased. The removal of Christian symbols (for secular services) and playing of tapes, compact discs or records will be completed as required.

Some staff may have first aid skills, as mourners and visitors sometimes collapse whilst on the premises. The staff will also meet families wanting to preview the chapels and facilities prior to a cremation service. Throughout the day, staff will help visitors considering or searching for memorials, cremated remains' locations or any other enquiries.

The Cremation Process

The crematorium staff may all be qualified Cremator Technicians, and will operate the cremators on a rota. Modern cremators cost approximately £170,000 (2003) for a single unit, which will complete 800 – 1,000 cremations per year. The modern cremator must conform to the requirements of the Environmental Protection Act 1990, with strict limits on emissions. This influences the design of coffins. The Act also requires that only qualified cremator technicians operate the cremator. In view of environmental concern, the operation of cremators may be reviewed. This is due to the high cost of pre-heating each cremator for use, which requires considerable gas and creates emissions. To reduce this, it is logical to use fewer cremators, for longer periods of time. To facilitate this, it would be necessary to change the Code of Practice to allow each cremation to be completed within 24 hours, rather than on the working day on which the service took place.

The cremator operator will transfer coffins manually, at the finish of each service, from the catafalque and through to the crematory. The nameplate on the coffin will be checked against the identity card, and if correct, the coffin will be cremated. If there are identity anomalies, checks will be completed to ascertain why. The most common reason is that people use different names, or nicknames, and these can be put on coffin nameplates. The coffin will be cremated as soon as a cremator is ready, which may be immediately or later during the day. If the cremated remains are to be collected on the same day, and perhaps buried in the afternoon, the cremation will be programmed early. The coffin will be pushed manually into the cremator, off a bier; or with some cremators, a charging machine will carry the coffin into the cremator and lower it into position. The charging process can be witnessed by relatives, if desired. The cremator will have been pre-heated to 850°C prior to this stage, and using various gas and air jets, the cremation will progress. In the most modern cremators, the process will be micro-processor controlled and little operator attention is needed. The principal aim is to maintain temperatures and reduce emissions, with no emission of smoke.

Each cremation will take about 1 hour 20 minutes, and will attain in excess of 1,000°C. At the completion of the process, the cremated remains will be raked out manually, cooled and processed through a machine that reduces them to a fine, granular state. The identity card, which has followed through the process, will be placed with the cremated remains. These will be placed in accordance with the instructions of the applicant for cremation. The choices available are described in the Charter item **Cremated Remains and Memorialisation**. When the remains are either buried or taken away, the identity card will be signed and returned to the office. The location will be recorded in the Cremation Register and the card filed with the other cremation forms. The receipt of the signed card signifies the completion of the process.

The above process illustrates a gas cremator, and it should

be noted that a small number of electric cremators are now in use. These operate in a similar manner, with gas jets being replaced by radiant electric elements.

Baby or Infant Cremations

The details in this item apply to baby or infant deaths, with a few exceptions. Often, a parent will carry the coffin of a young child and bearers are not needed. It is also necessary to consider that with the cremation of a small child, there may be no cremated remains available after the cremation. This is because the cartilaginous structure can be entirely cremated, leaving no residue. This fact can upset the parents and a procedure for warning them has been formulated for use by crematoria. Many details in the Charter item **Baby and Infant Graves** apply to a cremation funeral, and should be considered. The choice of cremation container may be restricted on safety grounds, based on the need to place this manually into an extremely hot cremator.

Although hospital funeral arrangements for stillbirth and other baby deaths often designate burial, some allow only cremation. It is extremely important not to cremate stillborn babies or children of those parents whose faiths oppose cremation. In some hospital arrangements, all the foetal deaths and stillborn babies will be taken to the crematorium periodically, say each month. A service will be conducted, to which all the parents are invited, and the cremation will follow. Each cremation must be individual, as the Code of Practice still applies. This practice is not necessarily approved, although in view of the absence of burial space and reducing resources for hospitals, the ability for these matters to be determined locally is necessary. It is important that these decisions are taken after consultation with charities and support groups involved in such bereavement.

Chapel of Rest

This is a room, which may be in the crematorium building or adjacent, for storing coffined bodies. It is used after the body has been collected from the place of death or mortuary, placed in a coffin, and transported to the crematorium. This may be early on the day of the funeral, or some days previously. The benefit is that the coffin can be moved manually to the main chapel for the service, without using a hearse. Combined with the family and mourners using their own cars, it also avoids the cost of hiring black mourning cars. This chapel is used by funeral directors, some of whom have no coffin storage facilities, and families carrying out funerals without a funeral director. A fee is usually charged for the use, based on the period the body is retained. The family may be able to view the body privately, by arrangement.

Fees

A list of fees is available from your Charter member, which would typically include:

- The cremation fee (average £291.00 for an adult in 2003) which is usually inclusive of all administrative work, Medical Referee, use of chapel, organist and/or electronic music, the cremation and placing of the cremated remains in the Garden of Remembrance.

- An increased cremation fee for non-residents of the area, where this applies.

- Fees for caskets and other containers for removing cremated remains.

- A fee to send cremated remains by a secure carrier, anywhere in the UK.

- The fee for usage of a Chapel of Rest if available.

- Fee to place cremated remains from other crematoria, in the Garden of Remembrance.

- Fees for memorials available at the crematorium.

- The fees that relate to a funeral which are paid by funeral directors on behalf of their clients, and a receipt given. These payments can be checked by the Applicant for Cremation, with any Charter member. If a funeral director is not used, the fees can be paid by any individual.

Cremated Remains and Memorialisation

Some people wish to place the cremated remains in a favourite spot, perhaps a hill or coastal location. The law offers no restrictions although, in theory, you need the permission of the landowner. The crematorium will place the cremated remains in an inexpensive container, from which you can scatter them. These containers might be plastic, aluminium or cardboard, and will contain the 5-7 lb (2kg) of remains from each cremation. Some people scatter them, or inter them in a casket, in their garden. In this case it is important to consider that you may ultimately leave your house, or die yourself. If the cremated remains are your partner or child, you will then be unable to place your cremated remains together in the same location.

Other people may wish to place the cremated remains in a cemetery, a churchyard or another crematorium, perhaps in an area where the family have their roots. You need to check on the type of container acceptable at the location. Churchyards generally will not accept plastic, metal or wood containers, preferring the remains to be placed in the earth without a container. Biodegradable cardboard caskets are now available which might prove acceptable. Most cemeteries will accept a wood casket. You should note that if a

Monthly Gardens

The grounds of Carlisle's crematorium are planted with "monthly gardens" – which are beds where the planting scheme has been designed to come into its own and look at its best during a certain month of the year. This underlines seasonal, cyclical, local rhythms related to the weather. The snowdrops appear, or the heathers bloom and the berries ripen on the rowan tree...

Since many people make a visit to the graveside or a memorial on the anniversary of a death, this ensures that the site always looks its best on these occasions.

It is usual for a surviving widow or widower to request that their ashes be placed alongside their partner's in the monthly garden, irrespective of the month during which the second death occurred.

Families creating a memorial area at home, in the garden, where ashes may be scattered or buried, might wish to bear this in mind and choose to plant a tree or bulbs, or perennials, which will flower on the anniversary of the death.

family grave, which has been used for burial, is full, it may still accept a considerable number of cremated remains. Recording these on the memorial on the grave may use up all the inscription space. You can usually overcome this by adding inscribed vases, or flat tablets, or similar, in front of the existing memorial.

Many people prefer to keep the cremated remains where the cremation took place. This ensures that they are secure and enables them to use the memorial facilities that are available.

The grounds of the crematorium form what is called the Garden of Remembrance. It is not consecrated, but is dedicated to the dead of all religions and non-believers. It is important that the grounds are attractive and welcoming, offering solace and solitude, when these are needed by visitors. Logically, wide open lawns with very little planting would not be suitable. The Garden of Remembrance is a memorial in itself and when cremated remains are placed in the grounds, it is your decision as to whether you need an actual memorial of your own.

Some bereaved people benefit from a feeling of attachment and ownership of the grounds, where the cremated remains of their loved ones lie. A memorial in the form of a tree or shrub

An Award Winning Cemetery

There is one large, well-managed cemetery in the north of Carlisle with a well-kept area for the babies' graves. In his wisdom, the manager has regulated the maximum size of memorials. This is the only constraint. There are granite teddy bears, hearts – not traditional imagery. Couples most often losing a baby are young, low income families, and this restriction means that for a very modest sum they can get a "proper" dignified memorial from the mason. In addition to the fresh flowers, there are soft toys and hand-made toys placed as offerings. The place has a sense of a collection of personal shrines, to children who lived often for only one or two days. Some families over a couple of years have lost more than one infant.

These graves tend to be visited daily at first, then weekly for the first year.

The Dead Good Funerals Book

planting scheme may offer this. This feeling of attachment can be so great that people leave bequests in their wills to the crematorium.

The bereaved want to feel that the crematorium management cares, and has credibility and integrity. Formal gardens, bedding, manicured lawns, ecology areas and wildlife pools are evidence of care and competence. Theming the grounds seems popular, including monthly gardens, heather gardens, cherry groves and such like. These all offer a sense of place, and well-being, to those who use the grounds. Visiting the crematorium, placing flowers and remembering anniversaries, can be therapeutic following a bereavement.

The choice available for placing the cremated remains may be considerable. The placement is usually free of charge, if the cremation took place at that crematorium. Either strewing (spread over the surface) and/or burial may be available. Strewing often results in the remains being visible on the surface, which can distress some visitors. If you wish to attend the placing of the cremated remains, check that this is possible.

Generally, a burial or strewing of cremated remains in the gardens does not offer people a specific location, only the approximate position in which they are placed. You are unable to put a vase on or otherwise mark the position, and you cannot recover the cremated remains. This is not satisfactory for some people, who might need a memorial on which they can see an inscription on every occasion that they visit.

Memorials

The range of memorials available varies greatly between crematoria and these should be considered carefully before a decision is made.

Any memorial will be an additional expense and is not covered by the fees paid for cremation. The simplest form of memorial is the Book of Remembrance, which can be viewed only on the anniversary date, although some schemes are available which enable you to view every day for a few years. The entries are done in calligraphy, by artists, on high quality paper. Flower emblems, crests, badges and other artwork can be included. This memorial is usually displayed in cabinets in a Hall of Remembrance. At a few crematoria, a basic entry in the Book of Remembrance may be free of charge.

Other types of memorial may be available which are placed in the grounds. These may include designs that enable you to place an inscription as well as placing the cremated remains beneath or by the memorial. The Memorial Wall, Columbaria and Kerb plaque schemes may give you this facility. These schemes are ideal for retaining cremated remains until the death of a second partner, when both cremated remains can be placed together.

Wishbone House

Wishbone House is a contemporary garden pavilion designed and constructed in 2000 by Duncan Copley for Welfare State International, through a commission from English Heritage.

It is a space for new ceremonies such as baby namings, betrothals, memorial gatherings and other personal or public rites of passage.

Handcarved from native hardwoods, including holly, elm, lime and larch, mostly sourced in the Lake District, Wishbone House is designed to underpin the making and marking of wishes in the setting of a peaceful sanctuary.

Shelter is provided by ten oak ribs which support an undulating willow wall, reminiscent of boats, forest clearings and ribbed caves. The structure is portable and may be embellished with flowers, foliage, flags, enhanced with poetry, songs, music and food. As the focus for outdoor gatherings, the space may be extended with processional approaches and fires in braziers.

NO NEED

Raymond Carver

I see an empty place at the table.
Whose? Who else's? Who am I kidding?
The boat's waiting. No need for oars
or a wind. I've left the key
in the same place. You know where.
Remember me and all we did together.
Now, hold me tight. That's it. Kiss me
hard on the lips. There. Now
let me go, my dearest. Let me go.
We shall not meet again in this life,
so kiss me good-bye now. Here, kiss me again.
Once more. There. That's enough.
Now, my dearest, let me go.
It's time to be on the way.

PART THREE
IMPROVEMENTS AND ALTERNATIVES

A dozen ways to improve funeral arrangements at very short notice

1   Think about where the funeral should be. It does not have to be in church (unless you want a C of E service). It could be a small gathering at home, at a community centre, in the cricket pavilion, outside in a garden or woodland.

2   Think about whether you need a minister of religion or celebrant, or whether you have somebody who could lead the funeral ceremony. Make no mistake. This is a sensitive and difficult function. It must be someone experienced enough to maintain their composure throughout the proceedings.

3   Pick up the telephone and speak to the manager of the crematorium or cemetery or a representative from any church or chapel you may be using. Tell them when you are coming for the funeral. Tell them if you have any particular requests.

4   Decide if you would like extra time for the service for any reason and negotiate a suitable time of day. Ask about any extra charges.

5   Find time to visit the place in advance and talk through with a member of staff what will happen when and where. Make sure you ask what the normal proceedings are (curtains close automatically? Coffin glides away? Coffin remains?) and be sure you are comfortable with this. Find out the limits of what is possible.

6   Look at the artefacts displayed in the space (crucifix etc). If you do not want them, ask for them to be removed or covered up. Ask them to show you what lights are usually on.

7   Consider what you might bring in from home and talk to the manager about this. Candles, a special cloth or banner to drape the coffin, a lantern, decorations, a photograph in

HOLDING ON
John Fox

When your friends die,
when the mist clings to the mountain,
lingering it seems for ever.
When in the small hours
shadows stalk;
then is a time for poetry.

Will o' the whispering candles
recur,
glimmering in the rawness.

Burning suffering.
Spluttering "Love".
So that from all that lonely bruising
we can be more.
Many hands will hold us
as we continue
to hold each other.

Across the black lake
pinpoints of light are holding too.
Here is Love weaving her thread,
weaving her soft blanket to cushion
the unfathomable cradle.

The Dead Good Funerals Book

a frame, any characteristic personal object belonging to the person who has died. Who will bring it? When?

8   How is the seating arranged? In a modern crematorium the seats are not always fixed, therefore there is no need for straight rows with everyone looking at each others' backs. Maybe a semicircle, or a circle would be good for a moderate size of congregation. If you request this, help the staff by agreeing to be the last funeral of the day, or the first.

9   Do you want any music? The sound of the organ is inextricably linked for most of us with church services. Only book the resident organist if that is what you want. In some crematoria their services come free, and the use of the cassette player or CD player is charged for. In others, it is the other way round. You may prefer your own choice of pre-recorded music. Check what playback facilities exist. For the entry/arrival it is usual to have 6-8 minutes of music; for the committal only a few bars are needed; exit music usually lasts about five minutes. Label each tape or CD clearly showing what is to be played when. Tapes should be set so your piece of music starts immediately it is switched on. Getting the music right is important. It is a good idea to make this the job of one person who will get there early. If you want no recorded music, you must say so, otherwise it could be switched on automatically as you arrive. If you want live music, read the section **How to find a Musician**.

10   Think about individual contributions to the funeral service, such as one or two people getting up to give an address, read a poem or tell a favourite story. Remember the film **Four Weddings and a Funeral** and the powerful W H Auden poem "Stop all the Clocks"? Make definite arrangements that are clearly understood. Give a brief written running order to anyone involved. Avoid using microphones if you possibly can. If you must, then arrange a practice.

11   If you would like to invite everyone to do something at the funeral, ie gather at the gate to walk together to the graveside instead of driving, or throw a single flower into the grave, make sure you mention this clearly in the newspaper announcement. You will not have time to telephone everyone. It is possible for a few people to get involved practically after a burial by filling in the grave themselves, but only if you have requested this in advance, so they can supply enough

shovels. Discuss these plans with the cemetery/crematorium manager *and* your funeral director. The best and simplest thing you can do, in our opinion, is to *take the flowers out of the cellophane wrapping* for a start.

12 Consider some ideas for the gathering afterwards. You may encourage everyone to bring along their photographs or souvenir albums to display on a table for people to browse through together. This helps to break the ice and talk through memories of the person who has died, or build bridges between relatives whose lives have drifted apart. And don't be afraid to get out your camera or camcorder to record this get-together. This last scene of the family album is usually the one that is missing. But before you do any of these things read the next section ....

But what about the relatives?

If there is one golden rule for people organising their own namings, weddings or funerals it must be "Remember to find time to talk to the relatives about your intentions beforehand". You will be busy organising so much that it is easy to overlook this, but it can be all in vain and end up a disappointment, if the nearest relatives do not feel included, at least in their understanding of what the ceremony is about, what is so important and why it includes the elements it does. People are creatures of habit and feel safe at a 'traditional' funeral or wedding, for example. If they feel lost or unsure – even about where to stand – they might feel less than positive in sharing your special moment.

But ... once you sit down together and talk about what matters, why it's important to you to do it this way, or in this special place, that makes so much difference. Even if they are not being invited to say or do something, they will feel more 'ownership' and involvement; they might even become "the authority" for more distant relatives to whom you will not speak directly.

It sometimes involves making a special journey in order to have this meeting, but it is so worthwhile. We have heard elderly relatives (who, remember, will have attended *many* weddings or funerals) say afterwards that it was "so moving ... so special ... I'll never forget it ..." because it was unique and personal, however simple.

The Dead Good Funerals Book

Recommendations for Improvement in Current Practice

1   When someone dies at home, keeping the body in the house may be positive and comforting for some families, depending on the circumstances of the death and on the house or flat, but harder for a single person left to cope unsupported. The opportunity to spend time over the leave-taking on familiar territory, to exclude strangers from handling the body and to decide what clothes will be worn in the coffin can all contribute to making the funeral personal. There are very few technical problems with keeping a body in the house for three days or so, as long as a cool room can be provided. Help with laying out can be provided by a district nurse.

What is needed is a change in the present attitude from funeral directors who automatically whisk the body away. Many people will want this service, but the choice, for the body to stay at home should be there, and as ever, it is better if the preference has been thought about in advance and research done into local sources of help.

2   Scheduling was the issue that people felt most strongly about. Mourners should have as much time in the crematorium as they need. There should be no overlap, no queues. In an ideal situation no funeral should see another funeral. Funeral directors may well throw up their hands in horror, but it is important to ask in whose favour are the schedules drawn up. If you particularly want a funeral early in the morning, or in the evening at sunset, or at a weekend, why should it not be possible? The current regimentation comes from an outmoded attitude towards providing a service. We currently get buried or cremated Monday to Friday, 9-5 or more like 10-4. It uncannily parallels the extraordinary number of babies born in hospital within the same shifts.

3   Flexibility in layout could be offered not so much in chapels but in crematoria, since many modern ones do not have fixed seating. It could be rearranged from the formal rows all facing the front, to a semicircle or horseshoe, or a circle even where mourners can make eye contact with each other. It could be removed altogether, to accommodate cultural and religious

diversity such as kneeling on the carpet to pray, or sitting in a circle on the floor, or wilder options altogether – like dancing! Temporary decorations, bringing in personal objects for the service, should be permitted. With co-operation and goodwill this could work, because it is always going to be a minority choice. People asking for a longer time could reasonably be offered the last appointment of the day, to facilitate preparation beforehand and putting things straight afterwards.

Hi-tech sounds and images at a Funeral?

I had always been fascinated by tape-slide shows and had recently produced a few when my mother became seriously ill. As I drove back from the hospital – having just been told that she was likely to die within the next few months – a vision appeared in my mind of a short tape-slide show about her life being shown at her funeral service. I was very moved by this idea and tears came into my eyes just thinking about it.

In the weeks which followed I allowed all sorts of barriers to come before me: (a) It would be impossible to get the equipment set up, the show over, and everything dismantled again within the typical crematorium 30 minute slot; (b) it probably would be impossible to blackout the building; (c) friends and relatives expecting "the usual kind of funeral" might find the whole thing rather tasteless or upsetting. In addition I was having to support my dying mother and my father who was looking after her ... it all seemed too much.

However, Christmas was within a month and I decided that I would make the show anyway, as a gift for my Mum. So I raided my parents' loft and copied dozens of family photographs on to slides. My original idea had been to include spoken word pieces but I didn't have time for this so I decided to use just one piece of music as background. It quickly came to me what it should be. My mother had learnt the piano as a child and she would always impress us as children by playing the first 20 bars of the "Blue Danube Waltz". In reality, she couldn't actually play anything else! I went out and bought a copy. It was absolutely perfect in that it had a tentative beginning that went with childhood photographs, an increasingly rousing section which went brilliantly with photos of my Mum in the prime of her life (getting married, having children etc), and a very tender ending which seemed to match photographs of her with grandchildren and old friends. The whole piece of music seemed to be like a life in itself – it felt as if it had been God-given for my purpose. I put together the sequence and showed the final product to my mother at Christmas. She immediately burst into tears and said that it was "horrid"

4   Support for the DIY funeral service and the needs of the arrangers should be offered. This may include turning off the recorded music and removing the religious artefacts visible in the church. "At the end we said no music specifically and they played piped music."

5   Regulations about memorials could be relaxed, to permit a wider choice of materials, less control of design, more freedom to make a hand-crafted (non-standard) memorial

and she was surprised that I didn't have a final photo of her in her box! Although she never mentioned it again I did feel from talking to her during her last few days that it had helped her in reviewing her own life story.

When she died six weeks later I decided that I couldn't cope with all the hassle of trying to get the show into the crematorium chapel. I felt that it could be a lot of effort and at the end of the day I might just end up with a lot of upset funeral-goers. However, my sister and I did have quite an input into the funeral service and many people remarked on what an upbeat event it had been.

The night before I had decided that I would offer the tape-slide show as an option at the gathering after the ceremony. So I set it up in an upstairs bedroom. Slightly nervously, I toured the room inviting people upstairs to see some pictures – I didn't know quite how to describe it. In the event we had three packed houses. Just about everyone who saw the ten-minute show was absolutely ecstatic and a number of them came up to me and said how moved they had been by it. Several people were very pleased to hear that my Mum had seen the show herself before her death. The reaction was such that I almost wished that I had stuck to my original vision of showing it at the crematorium. Although a couple of people had declined a viewing saying that they wouldn't be able to handle it I felt that such people would have been swept along with the others if it had been part of the main event.

Sound synchronised with images in an audio-visual presentation can be a very potent force. Although I didn't make any attempt to involve my mother in the making of this production I can imagine that it could be a very positive way for a person who had come to terms with their death to make a real input into their own funeral ceremony.

The technology has come a long way since then. It's now possible to run a sophisticated presentation using a laptop computer and a data projector and this means that set-up time can be dramatically reduced.

Jonathan How

The Dead Good Funerals Book

in wood or stone carving, or maybe a durable mosaic. These objects have a place, made as an act of love and very often made to a high standard. Why should machined slabs of alien granite in marble with computer generated lettering constitute the aesthetic that is held up for everyone to conform to? The use of natural pieces of local stone will offer a habitat for lichen and mosses which bring their own beauty. It might also help to keep a small quarry going, in preference to the exploitative trade of importing shiploads of marble at rip-off prices from third-world countries – the source that most monumental masons use. Hand-carved lettering may not be immaculate, but it retains the human touch.

A Leading Example

Carlisle Crematorium is given as a model of current good practice in the funerals industry. It won the Natural Death Handbook Award 2004 for the Best Crematorium and is also highly placed using the Best Value Assessment Process devised by Ken West for the Institute of Cemetery and Crematorium Management (ICCM) which involves self assessment against the Charter for the Bereaved.

Carlisle states 'Our attitude is one of complete openness, giving the bereaved complete access to the information they need in order to obtain a meaningful funeral. There is no commercial pressure or bias towards so-called conventional funerals'. The service offers both traditional and environmental options. The cemetery grounds are comprised of four different areas: the peace garden is bedded out and highly maintained providing the principal view from the Hall of Remembrance. The woods are for those who prefer a return to nature and dislike high maintenance regimes, the memorial wall offers a cremation memorial option and the monthly gardens are planted to a seasonal pattern.

They accept homemade and biodegradable coffins, body-bags and shrouds and offer cold storage for the body for a limited period. Extra bearers can also be supplied to help the family. The Chapel is non-denominational with flexible seating. Their standard price is £305, with an extra 40 minutes being bookable without further charge.

Using the ICCM method the City of London service comes out top. They provide a good but rather expensive service. Their services include open days, a choice of 5 chapels and transport around the cemetery.

The Dead Good Funerals Book

6   The industry codes of practice which have been drawn up in consultation with the Office of Fair Trading are intended to raise standards of service and give consumers access to low-cost means of seeking redress. Responsibility for publicising them and enforcing them lies with the trade associations. But codes can only have value if they are demonstrably taken seriously and complied with. Key requirements – offering price lists, written estimates and the right to a basic funeral (removal of the body to the Chapel of Rest, a simple coffin, the hearse plus one car) – are not being observed. It seems some funeral directors do not see the codes as relevant to the way they do business. In some parts of the country funeral directors believe their clients would feel insulted if they gave them a written estimate.

There is more formal intervention possible, to prevent the codes being dismissed as worthless, such as a price marking order or referral to the Monopolies and Mergers Commission, but the Office of Fair Trading prefers that the impetus for improvement will come swiftly, from within the funerals industry and trade associations. The primary responsibility for price transparency and for providing a simple funeral lies with funeral directors, who must lessen the information gap about what is available.

Recommendations to Local Authorities

1   There is a need for printed information setting out the choices available to people: burial, cremation, natural burial, together with details of options for coffins, shrouds, memorials. This should give straightforward unbiased advice. Do we have to have a funeral? Do we have to use a funeral director? What does a 'simple funeral' consist of? Can I be buried anywhere I want? ... and printed in LARGE print, also available on audiotape for visually-impaired people.

2   These leaflets should be widely available. Start at the Registrar's office, it's the one place everyone must go after a death; also health centres, hospitals, clinics, residential homes, libraries, post offices, community centres, Citizens' Advice Bureaux, churches, drop-in centres, family centres, schools, further education and community education centres. Responsibility

for distributing these leaflets to clients should be part of the agenda of health authorities and social welfare agencies, especially those for the elderly. The voluntary sector, such as Age Concern, already does a great deal, with their excellent booklets. Targeting organisations like Women's Institutes, Townswomen's Guilds, The Lions, Rotary Clubs, Round Table must prompt discussion at local level and exert pressure to bring about change if local funeral directors or cemetery managers are inadequate or inflexible. There are many fine grassroots organisations of people already coming together around death and bereavement. See listings in **The Natural Death Handbook**.

3 Information on new prayers, services, readings, alternative liturgies should be easily available for people seeking a secular or DIY funeral, coupled with book lists and information on where to find celebrants, musicians, artists. Carlisle and Croydon for example, have this information available.

4 There is a need for training programmes for celebrants and training packages available to firms of funeral directors and local authority staff to support them in responding to changing attitudes and to give confidence in re-appraising aspects of their service and introducing changes and wider choices. This must cover environmental awareness, design, the needs of younger people ...

Training for Celebrants

Most people need a celebrant to conduct secular services, as an alternative to the clergy, where conflicts of integrity occur. In Australia and Canada you find registered celebrants in the Yellow Pages. The authority is vested in the person, not in the person in a specified building, as in the UK. This shift in policy opens up choice immensely.

What knowledge and qualities does a celebrant need for the creation and presentation of secular ceremonies which are tailored to each situation? In our opinion, quite a lot. A programme of study for celebrants and funeral officiants covers both personal development and professional practice. It needs to include an understanding of the history and origins of rites of passage, the role and importance of ceremony today and cultural awareness. Basic competencies need to include interpersonal skills and knowledge of groups, organisation and business skills, expertise in communication and public presentation, structuring of ceremony and writing the words. In addition, development of resource materials, maintenance of professional networks, evaluation and assessment.

Welfare State International's rites of passage training programme takes place at Lanternhouse, our Centre for the Celebratory Arts in Ulverston, Cumbria. Two levels of study: a one-week introductory course that examines the philosophy and practicality of creating ceremonies and celebrations; an advanced course of one week for celebrants to deepen their experience and professional practice. These summer schools, led by Gilly Adams and Sue Gill, are a mix of theory and practice and include visits, case studies, expressive arts workshops, collaborative group work and opportunity for individual research in the specialist library of books and videos. Over the years, participants have suggested the following personal qualities that a celebrant would be expected to possess: integrity and sincerity, clarity, tact, listening skills, adequate maturity and life experience as the basis of good judgement, a concept of service, grace and poise, being alive to the here and now, stamina and a sense of humour.

Demand for ceremonies is increasing, as it should be in an increasingly secular nation. The number of funerals conducted by British Humanist Association (BHA) celebrants is rising year on year, growing from 3,000 in 1998 to 6,925 in 2002. Since 2002 there has been a Community Services Officer at the BHA. Part of their remit is to support and develop the ceremonies network through improving recruitment, training and appraisal procedures as well as supporting individual celebrants. Demand for weddings and namings is lower, averaging at about 300 namings per year and a similar number of weddings, including 50 gay weddings. The BHA runs courses to train and accredit individuals who wish to become Humanist celebrants or officiants. Some officiants conduct funerals and related ceremonies only, others will take on all types of ceremonies and some who call themselves celebrants choose to take weddings and namings. Typically the BHA train 36 funeral officiants and twelve celebrants a year and have a rolling register of around 200 people available to conduct ceremonies. Other training in the UK is available from the International Federation of Celebrants (affiliated to the Australian Federation of Civil Celebrants Inc).

Searching for a
new way forward

1   Alternative ceremonies are really needed. New liturgies, new prayers and poems and suitable readings, new forms of words for committal, particularly for a secular funeral. This could be a role for writers and poets who are interested in rites of passage and a context for their work. From their knowledge and research, they could take the best from the body of literature that exists, but be bold enough to add new work relevant to today. The writers would need to consider a range, from the thanksgiving at the end of a long and cherished life to stillbirth or the death of a child, or an unexpected death or after a suicide. Sudden death, violent death, unjust death, cruel death, not always peaceful death in secluded surroundings.

2   An aesthetic overhaul is needed of the design of coffins and funerary equipment; everything from the off-the-shelf 'gown' for ladies and gentlemen, fabrics and trimmings for lining coffins to the standard urns for ashes. We should encourage natural materials. Just ask to be shown what the choices are at your local funeral parlour. The bitter humour of Jan, a colleague, after seeing her father 'ready' in his coffin, in strange blue satin – half night, half day clothes – with a collar and floppy bow-tie to match – "My Dad wouldn't be seen dead in that ..." Art schools have a role to play here. If we want the Victorian aesthetic that's fine, but let's do it properly with real oak and dovetail joints not chipboard stapled together with a plastic veneer. How about a design competition with a national profile, for pleasing simple coffins and burial garments?

3   We need a major shift to create new spaces worthy of secular services; they are completely absent from our culture. These buildings should be fine enough in themselves architecturally and sited to offer indoor and outdoor possibilities for weddings, namings and funerals, in a landscaped space offering all services, including a space for gathering before or afterwards and for offering hospitality. In today's age of the camcorder, photogenic framing of the space will be essential, with inviting features, vistas and gateways, natural elements of stone, water, trees and plants. In Adelaide, South Australia, the crematorium is beautiful enough as a building and set among trees so that people choose to go there (with

their freelance celebrant) for open air wedding ceremonies. Were we to have secular spaces that we used for life enhancing experiences, such as naming of children, as well as for funeral ceremonies, it would truly bring death into life and underline the cyclical nature of our existence. Which Director of Social Services will be visionary enough to commission the first such building in the country? Why should it be left to the arts community with fewer means at its disposal? Such a model of good practice must enhance the status of an area.

Just as discerning people who value a richness of community life and who are able to choose, make an audit of a region before deciding to settle there – health, education, law and order, cultural and leisure provision, environmental awareness etc – this building could be another plus for enticing them to come, or to stay.

4   Green options must be on this agenda. Carlisle has pioneered natural burial as an option, in addition to traditional burial plots and cremation. The benefits to the community of a sensitively managed cemetery with plenty of trees and not too much mowing should be promoted, since they are considerable – potential bird reserves, wildlife havens for small mammals, butterflies, bats and insects. This offers an educational resource in the community (see **Natural Burial**).

5   It makes good sense to have a closer working between local authority arts units and bereavement services – in short, an arts policy for cemeteries. There is a tremendous role for landscape sculptors, rural artists, sculptors working in local materials, slate, stone, pebbles ... Storm damaged trees, for example, are an amazing resource, for sculptors. There is potential for imaginative and creative schemes – seating, pergolas, space definition, pathways, mosaics, gates and railings. Cemeteries contain many different areas – war graves, lawn graves, babies' graves, early Victorian monuments, paupers' unmarked graves, cremated remains' graves. This links particularly with educational projects, conservation work, and with schools. Decorum and suitability are most important here, to respect the needs of users of the cemetery. The company, Memorials by Artists, is a nationwide service which helps people to commission fine, individual memorials for churchyard, cemetery, garden or public space. Each memorial represents a unique response to a specific request.

Helpful Officials

Carlisle

"No-one can state precisely what we should do to have a 'good' funeral – there is no doubt that the best, most satisfying funerals are those where the deceased considered his/her funeral prior to death and made arrangements to achieve their wishes."

Ken West added in an address he prepared for Welfare State International's first Funerals weekend: "What about the current state of our funerals? Well, I cannot state with certitude that all our current funeral practices are wrong. Nor that they fail to meet the needs of the living. But, I can state positively that specific groups are not able to obtain satisfactory funerals. These are people that require a green funeral, those that require a cheap funeral, and those who want a "different" funeral. When I say different, I mean a funeral that is not processed, routine, bland! I can state, unequivocally, that if you have seen one funeral then you have seen them all. The influence of such bland funerals on the depression, the guilt, confusion, anger and aggression that arise with bereavement today is difficult to quantify.

"The funeral is a focal point, a public ceremony, a parting and, of course, many other things. The problem, I believe, is that a meaningful funeral can only occur if it has been thought about in advance. Otherwise, as a "crisis" arrangement, you are wholly unable to control the event and find yourself manipulated. The manipulators are the crematorium, who might give you a twenty-minute slot, the funeral director who must achieve eight funerals that day, the vicar who has done twenty funeral services that week. In other words, you simply get sucked into a process. A clinical body disposal system. This system can look slick and efficient, but is it what we want?

"Perhaps this is acceptable to the majority? I prefer to think not. I believe that the individuality of each person should be celebrated in some way at their funeral. This requires more education, such as this course, so that people are empowered to control their own funerals. The influence of commercialism and established values, must be reduced. We must create more consumer awareness and more consumer power."

His helpful notes on Funeral Arrangements – **Burial in Carlisle** – carry an introduction stating they are intended to help the bereaved understand their rights and complete as little or as much of the funeral arrangements as they wish, even to carrying out the funeral without a funeral director. The notes are intended to widen choice and help the bereaved and others obtain a satisfying funeral. They remind people gently to be sure they are offered a price list by their funeral director, and to consider what 'container' they prefer – a traditional coffin, a biodegradable coffin or a shroud. They offer a natural burial service – see section on **Natural Burials**.

You can provide your own music in the chapel if you wish, provide your own funeral flowers or alternatives, eg rosemary for remembrance. You can introduce symbolic acts, ie place some personal mementoes in the coffin beforehand; invite mourners each to throw a single flower into the grave during the service (protocol note: discuss with the Minister if you are using one); devise your own funeral service, but be sure you have someone who can deliver it at the funeral; you can consult examples of secular services available at the office.

London Borough of Richmond

The Cemeteries that are managed by the London Borough of Richmond are Charter for the Bereaved Members. The Cemeteries staff will offer help and advice to ensure funerals are as personal as possible. They are happy to meet with families to show them the different options available. They have areas where traditional memorials can be placed and encourage individual memorials. There are several unique memorials from wooden dolphins to carved boulders. There is a natural burial area, where there are no memorials at all. Children from the local school planted hundreds of bluebell bulbs in this area. There are also different options for the burial of cremated remains.

The cemeteries' service offer their own encouraging and supportive guide to family-arranged funerals in their cemeteries. They can help you to find a biodegradable coffin from managed forests; wicker, bamboo, cardboard coffins and burial shrouds rather than coffins made from tropical hardwoods. Homemade coffins are also accepted. Coffins can be brought to the cemetery in a van, estate car, horse-drawn carriage, traditional hearse or other suitable method, for example in a motorcycle sidecar hearse. There is advice on carrying and lowering the coffin. The family are welcome to back-fill the grave if they wish, following the burial.

The cemetery chapels are available for funeral services and personal memorial services. There are music systems in all chapels. Services can also be held at the graveside and a gazebo-type shelter is available. Families are welcome to take the service themselves. The cemetery staff can help you to produce an order of service sheet and you can borrow books with readings and poems from them. They can help you to find musicians, caterers and venues for refreshments. The cemetery office, toilets and chapels are accessible to everyone. The chapels are fitted with an induction loop. Wheelchairs are available.

There are memorial services held twice a year for all those buried in the cemeteries and a special service for babies and children is held annually.

For contact details see **Resources & Contacts**.

Education

Death and dying should be in the school curriculum, as part of "Citizenship". The more education, the more frequent the forum for debate, the more it is in our consciousness, the more empowered we can be in making suitable choices, and in influencing change from varied cultural standpoints. What is the youth culture angle on funerals, for example?

Studies of death and dying have a place across creative writing and literature studies, environmental science, consumer awareness, art and design, comparative religions, music, architecture, social history, political history, the history of medicine, business studies, heritage studies, design and technology ... even outdoor pursuits, given an imaginative approach. We live in South Cumbria, where outdoor pursuits are strong. Students pursue fell walking, orienteering and undertake practical survival exercises. Retracing old coffin routes across the landscape would meet all these needs, but have other 'outcomes' too. A closer understanding of social history, where people without a local graveyard were obliged to transport their dead in the coffin using a cart or sometimes only a packhorse to a distant burial ground which was a very serious and difficult expedition. Our local route, Torver to Conishead, is a distance of 16 miles over the fell. Imagine that in stormy winter weather, with floods, boggy roads, high hills and other difficulties frequently occuring. This is the stuff of local legends. Children need to be given the tools to understand their own environment and this includes death and dying. We need a broader, more contextual and ecological perspective, a holistic approach, yet also specific areas of study.

Natural Burial

Natural Burial is both an ancient tradition and a new idea, an extra choice being offered by some local authorities and private cemeteries.

In Carlisle, for example, the natural graves are in a field adjacent to the extensive Victorian cemetery. This land is specially dedicated for this sole purpose, with the possibility of extending the area for many decades to accommodate future demand. The burial area will be planned to re-create traditional oak woodland and the accumulating graves will remain forever in a newly created forest.

The management will encourage wild flowers and will create a habitat for wildlife – therefore it will not be mown in the traditional manner. Butterflies, insects, bats, small mammals and birds will benefit as the trees grow and the undergrowth develops.

Each natural grave will accept two burials side by side. They have been individually numbered and carefully recorded on plans to ensure that the graves can always be found as nature gradually creates the woodland over the years. After burial, the soil will be allowed to settle, then a small native oak tree will be planted and the grave covered with bluebell bulbs and wild flower seed. Family, friends and relatives are encouraged to return and do this themselves.

Biodegradable coffins are preferred, or shrouds, or coffins in natural wood (preferably reclaimed timber or wood from managed, sustainable forests). Standard chipboard coffins supplied by most funeral directors are also acceptable. Home-made coffins or containers may be used, so long as these are safe to handle. Cremated remains can also be buried in the natural burial area, and similar requirements will apply to caskets used to contain the ashes.

Some traditional cemeteries reserve burial areas for specific religions. This does not apply to Carlisle's natural burial ground. The dead of all faiths will be buried in the same area. Traditional funeral patterns do not have to be followed, and the funeral can be carried out with or without the guidance of a funeral director. There is encouragement and support for the relatives and friends wishing to arrange the burial themselves.

This choice is for those who want to get back in touch with a more natural way of dealing with death, and favour burial under a tree in a natural setting. Those with no relatives to care for a traditional grave and memorial, avoid the problem of a neglected site in the future.

As the Carlisle scheme is designed to benefit the environment, grave memorials are not allowed. This is because individual memorials demand grave visits, and the visitors would soon trample the wildflowers and habitat being created. Spiritually, the essence of the woodland would be destroyed. To allow some form of commemoration, a sheepfold has been constructed of recycled stone in the centre of the developing woodland. Stone plaques can be placed on the inside wall of the fold, and viewed from a wood, circular seat in the centre. This ensures that the memorials do not intrude on the natural appearance of the woodland.

There has been a huge upsurge in new natural burial sites in recent years, and close on 150 are now available. The conditions applied by the site owners vary greatly, and should be considered carefully. Many place the burials in glades between the trees and an individual tree is not planted. Others allow biodegradable wood memorials, providing these are not treated with chemical preservatives. Category "A" designated sites mow no more than twice each year, use native trees, and no stone memorials. Any site not meeting this standard will be classified as Category "B". They will do regular mowing beneath the trees and although this destroys many wildflowers and degrades the habitat, it does look neater and appeals to some people. In view of this movement away from creating wild woodland, the term "natural burial" rather than "woodland burial" has become the accepted description.

If this kind of burial interests you then ring your local council to see if they operate such a scheme. If not, ask them why not! There are several examples from around the country where pressure from an individual has been successful in getting one established.

Churchyard Re-use

In Britain our tradition has been to see the local churchyard fill up with graves over the years and then shut. That's it. Frozen forever at an historical point in the past, with no living connection with any local families, no visitors, no-one caring for the sometimes decrepit graves. A museum of the dead, an historical archive.

People using the church regularly for worship, for weddings, for christenings, for funerals or memorial services, or just walking through the graveyard, are not connected with reminders of the recent dead from their local communities. The fresh flowers and tributes are to be seen in bright abundance, but only in the vast municipal cemeteries, which are often miles away on the edge of town.

Groundbreaking Funeral Services

In the course of the development of a national network of secular celebrants WSI have identified several small independent companies offering specialist funeral services. A couple of examples from Devon and East Sussex:

"**green fuse** takes its inspiration from the flower as the universal symbol of life force from which we draw the great metaphors of birth, life, love and death. We believe we have created a wonderful and truly groundbreaking service at **green fuse** as we seek to integrate floristry and beautiful flowers with meaningful ceremony in a relaxed and informal setting where we give very practical advice and support to bereaved families.

Amongst the blossoms we act as independent funeral advisors and by opening up choices can help a family focus on the type of funeral they really want and how to go about organizing this. We are mindful of how difficult it can be to make decisions and choices about death. Using the best and most appropriate services available we can suggest simple and affordable ways to improve a funeral ceremony in order to comfort the bereaved, honestly acknowledge the person, and give them a heartfelt send-off from this world into whatever lies beyond."

ARKA – Original Funerals

"At **ARKA** we can help people feel comfortable and safe to make decisions about the funeral of a loved one. We offer advice and information about choosing alternative sites for burial and options for creative funeral services. We acknowledge diversity of religious and spiritual beliefs. **ARKA** can organise the provision of a Minister or Celebrant and help you with as much or as little personal involvement in the funeral as required and advise on all the legalities."

ARKA also offer their range of colourful Ecopod coffins, designed and manufactured by Hazel Selene. Made entirely from recycled material, the eco-friendly pod is a safe and beautiful alternative to conventional coffins, available in a range of designs such as 'Doves in Flight' – dove design on dark blue hand-made mulberry and silk paper with matching carrying straps.

For contact details see **Resources & Contacts**

The National Funerals College

is a small not-for-profit group set up to stimulate better funeral practice. It has come up with the idea of a funeral adviser in organisations where people die – such as hospitals, hospices and care homes. This would be an existing member of staff or volunteer who, after training, would be able to supply impartial, well-informed and free information about funerals to dying people and those closest to them.

The idea was tested in a number of hospices and care homes and described in **Funeral Advisers: Is there a need?** by the project's director, Rose Heatley, (£5.00 including postage and packing from The National Funerals College).

Following this work, the hospice movement became further involved. Help the Hospices has run several one-day funeral information workshops for hospice staff, and published a 17-page booklet by Rose Heatley entitled **Providing Information About Funerals: issues and ideas for hospices**, (cost £5.00 from Hospice Information, tel: 0870 903 3903). Rose Heatley also compiled the first of two pilot issues of "Funeral Information Update" which can be downloaded from http://www.helpthehospices.org.uk/education/index.asp?submenu=2

The Update is for those outside the funeral industry who work with people who may need information about funerals and related matters.

In Belgium there is a non-authoritarian plan for re-use of graves which Dr Tony Walter describes in his book **Funerals and How to Improve Them**. Some people like the idea, some people hate it, we find. He writes about one village of Wommelgeus, which has a population of 5,000:

> "You used to be able to buy a plot in perpetuity, but that changed in 1971 ... they could see that their cemetery was getting full, so the village council determined, and now regularly reviews, the length of time for which you can rent, not buy, a grave. Say it is ten years. Tending the grave is your responsibility. If after ten years, you or other relatives are still tending the grave, you can pay for another ten years, and so on, until interest wanes. If after any ten year period you do not re-apply, a notice is pinned to the grave, giving you a year's notice. If you still do not re-apply, the grave is available to

be used again. This way, money is always coming in to maintain the cemetery, and there are always relatives willing and able to maintain individual graves."

The result? A guarantee of beautifully kept graves, no vandalism, good ecological practice, a counter to increased cremation and its environmental impact on the atmosphere. This re-use policy is self-regulating (fifteen years is the average documented grave attendance in Britain) and would bring the churchyard back as a viable community resource, along with the post office and the school,

"... a communal place of green and rest, where living and dead commune, where another time, another place, another spirit offer an oasis in the city."

Artists in Hospices

A small but growing number of celebratory artists are developing a role within hospices and palliative care. Their work is different from that of arts therapy or diversional activities, perhaps sitting between the two. The artists work alongside the residents, making work with or for them as a result of spending considerable time together. The collaboration supplies a new language through which individuals can express themselves, their lives, their illness and also their wider identities. It can provide a vessel for reflection or opportunities for communication which become forms of personal ceremony or ritual.

The work opens up a channel that often leads to and supports the discussion and planning by the individual of their funeral or memorial. This can be deeply beneficial to residents, their families and carers. The role of the artist working in this way can continue after a death, with the bereaved and the work of the care staff.

Rosetta Life is a unique artist-led organisation pioneering artists' contributions to palliative care. They have an ever-growing network of artists-in-residence in hospices enabling people with life-threatening illnesses and their families to explore their experiences through writing, music, video, photography, poetry and other art forms. They are working in partnership with hospices across the country creating a shared website for palliative care users, served by multi-media arts facilities at each site. Their work clearly illustrates the link between creative practice and spiritual development as an essential principle of holistic care.

And moreover, we could be offering back to people the chance, if they wished, to be buried in the ground where their neighbours and/or their ancestors, had been buried for possibly the last thousand years, and where their own family had maybe been going to witness their weddings, their baptisms and their funerals for say, the last fifty years. It could root us much more coherently to where we are on the planet. Given a choice between that and the option of a period or perpetuity on the ring road, we wonder how many would take up the former?

Biodegradable coffins

Most natural burial sites prefer the bereaved to choose a biodegradable coffin. To qualify in this sense, both the exterior and interior of the coffin must be capable of absorption into the soil. Sometimes, chipboard or MDF is advertised as "biodegradable", ignoring the fact that harmful resins bind the wood particles together, and will pollute the soil. The inside of these "traditional" coffins is also lined with plastic film.

Wicker coffins are often promoted as biodegradable. These, though, have an open weave design and may not include a non-plastic liner. Consequently, because funeral directors and others worry about body fluids or odour they fit their own plastic liners inside the wicker. This is the same plastic film as that used inside chipboard/MDF coffins. Some of the cardboard coffins are also routinely fitted with plastic film liners.

Taking out the sting! Heaven on Earth

"Heaven on Earth", the first Design-it-Yourself Life and Death shop in the country, has opened in Bristol.

The shop offers a design-your-own death package at half the costs of the conventional channels. Included is their "Embodiment Chest" which can be custom-made and decorated to suit interior colour schemes and be used as a bookcase, window seat or conventional storage chest until it's needed to store you!

The shop sells a whole range of coffins including Compakta cardboard coffins at £75. They also offer a 24-hour funeral arrangement service and green burials. The shop recently won an award from the Natural Death Centre who believe that one day every city will have a shop like this.

from Planetary Connections Autumn 1995

The Dead Good Funerals Book

The environmental objection to plastic liners includes concern about their impact on the decomposition of the body. It is suggested that the plastic liner retains rainfall permeating through the soil. This water could cover the body and prevent it decaying naturally. This would prevent the constituents of the body being slowly dissipated into the adjacent soil and absorbed by tree and other roots, the intended purpose of natural burial.

Ideally, cardboard coffins should have a water-based gel lining. Another excellent alternative is the bamboo coffins which have a specially designed woven cotton liner. This contains the body and ensures the entire coffin is biodegradable.

A lino-cut made by Catriona Stamp on the death of her father – who was a keen archer

How to make a
Shroud

What you will need:

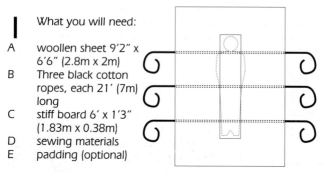

A   woollen sheet 9'2" x 6'6" (2.8m x 2m)
B   Three black cotton ropes, each 21' (7m) long
C   stiff board 6' x 1'3" (1.83m x 0.38m)
D   sewing materials
E   padding (optional)

The shroud is intended to replace a coffin. It cocoons the body in warm natural fibres rather than the chipboard and plastics used in modern coffins. It also avoids the waste of resources associated with coffin usage.

The body is laid on the board (together with padding if a smooth outline is required). The shroud is then folded over from one side, the ends folded in and the second side folded over the top. A few stitches can be made to hold the shroud in place.

This shroud design is known as the "Carlisle" Burial Shroud and is reproduced here courtesy of Ken West.

2 Lay the three cotton ropes on the floor.

3 Place the woollen sheet over the ropes and lightly stitch at the centre of each rope to prevent any movement.

4 Place the board in the centre on top of the woollen shroud.

Six bearers are ideal but four can manage without difficulty. If four are used, then the head-bearer should hold one end and the foot-bearer two ends to maintain an even balance.

The Dead Good Funerals Book

How to assemble a
Zimbabwean
Collapsible Coffin

This type of coffin doesn't have wooden sides or a wooden top. Just a wooden base which folds into thirds and a shroud which is attached to the base. It all folds down into a bag which can be slung over the shoulder and carried home on the bus! It has been tremendously popular in Africa where the price of conventional coffins is high and buses will not carry them. Now also available in the UK.

1 Remove the "box" (as it is called) from its bag.

2 Unfold the "box".

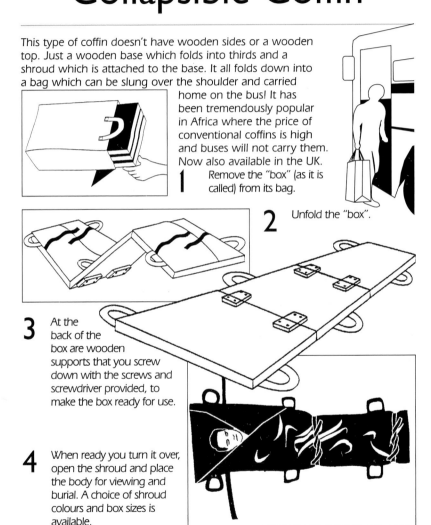

3 At the back of the box are wooden supports that you screw down with the screws and screwdriver provided, to make the box ready for use.

4 When ready you turn it over, open the shroud and place the body for viewing and burial. A choice of shroud colours and box sizes is available.

How to assemble a
Cardboard
Coffin

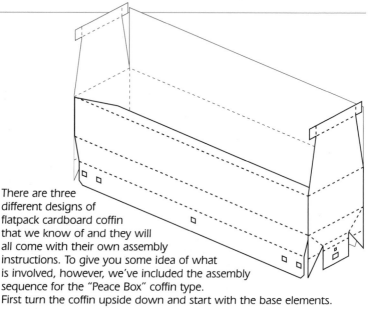

I There are three different designs of flatpack cardboard coffin that we know of and they will all come with their own assembly instructions. To give you some idea of what is involved, however, we've included the assembly sequence for the "Peace Box" coffin type.
First turn the coffin upside down and start with the base elements.

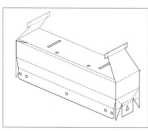

2

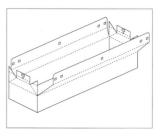

3 Now turn the coffin over and work on the top.

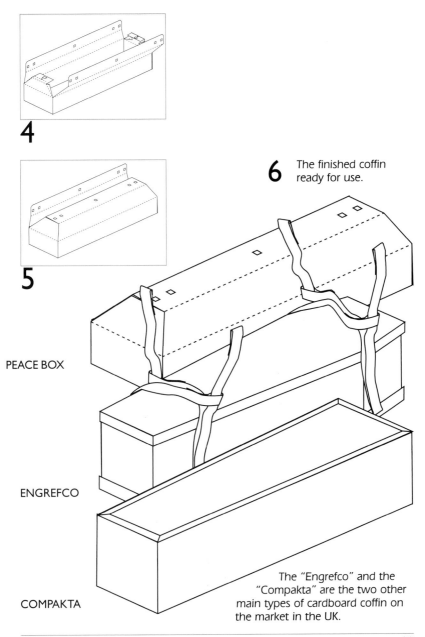

4

5

6 The finished coffin ready for use.

PEACE BOX

ENGREFCO

COMPAKTA

The "Engrefco" and the "Compakta" are the two other main types of cardboard coffin on the market in the UK.

SECULAR PRAYER

John Fox

Where will we be
a hundred years from now?
Will waves pound at the monument on the hill?
Will our Parish Bells toll sad beneath the sea?
When worms dance ecstatically
in the flower pots of our skulls
and our dust flickers in the setting sun,
where will we be?
May our children's children dip their fingers in a clear beck.
May they feel sunshine on skin free from blisters.
I hope the virus of war will have gone forever.
That all weapons will be banned
and that no shell will ever land again
on orphans in a bread queue
I wish for simple things
in tranquil corners
Where love prevails
and neighbours help each other.
Above all
May our evolution be compassionate and kind.

PART FOUR
A PERSONAL EXPLORATION OF
ATTITUDES TO DEATH

Mother

When my mother was cremated, she was stapled into
a chipboard coffin surrounded by a plastic frilly doily.
The priest started before we arrived. He kept tripping over
under the plaster model of a giant Jesus that was deeply
cracked across the chest. A Christmas crib was covered in
creased black rayon. Six professional female middle-aged
mourners all wore green hats. The priest wailed to them,
"If you don't come to church regularly, you'll go to Hell."
Lucy Fox, my Mother, didn't go to mass regularly.

> Oh, Lucy FOX.
> You were bad
> and you're in a BOX.

Nobody took the flowers out of the cellophane.
I think it was my job. I was her only son. However, the
steamed-up plastic became a strong image for me. Here were
tears for the ineptitude of our culture. I never forgave the
priest.

Father

When my father died the ceremony was better.
The undertaker worked hard. The coffin was in his front
room workshop, with the pliers and staple guns on the
sideboard. More doilies but at least, in the words of the
undertaker: "You can photograph father before the lid is
screwed down". Bill Hall (a friend, vicar and Chaplain to the
Arts) helped. Instead of the piped music I hired a 'cellist.
My father was a sea captain and the gutsy gentleness of
the 'cello playing "For those in peril on the sea" helped.
Bill held me in the eye and talked me down. Even if I wasn't a
Christian, here was human contact and real music instead of a
piped tape. A good funeral and a good priest.

Later at the ash scattering ceremony we could make an even more personal ceremony. My father's trade was in the North Sea. The Humber pilot ferried us out one misty morning up the estuary between tramp steamers at anchor near Spurn Point. To the strains again of "For those in peril ...", played this time by our family brass quartet, initially myself, Sue, and our two children (ten and eleven), I tipped his ashes in the estuary. I judged the wind right. The pilot lowered the flag and the Seamen's Chaplain said a prayer. It was unforgettable.

The urn had been difficult. The undertaker gave us it in a faked bronze plastic cannister like a half-gallon oil container. It sat in our cellar for a year. When we worked abroad I left it with a friend in case the house burned down. How big is an urn? How heavy? How wide the lid? Is it made of wood or clay?

A potter friend who specialised in throwing decorative slipware helped. Many cultures buried their ashes in urns. Sometimes the pot is buried vertically. Sometimes upside down. As it happened my father loved biscuits and was a heavy pipe smoker. As a small child I can remember finding his biscuit barrel in his ship's cabin. But every urn we made came out looking like either a biscuit barrel or a tobacco jar! Now I wouldn't worry. In fact I would welcome a domestic association rather than meaningless, fashionable or authoritarian ritual imposed by some-one else's tradition, values or aesthetic. Why not a Toby Jug even?

In the end we made it a bit like a small circular beehive (see photograph on back cover). A big flat bottom, 12" across, to rest on the prow of the pilot cutter. A wide lid, 6" across, for the ejection of ashes and a silk handle the colour of clouds and waves to tie it on with. And a poem. In white slip, on the dark brown of the pot's surface, we inscribed:

> "The last voyage of Captain Fox, MBE.
> May his spirit be at peace with the sea."

Making the grief concrete was memorable and healing for us all but it had been very hard to start.

Mick

But then another friend dies. A painter, a lover of impressionist sunshine and delicate spring flowers. A humourist. A boozer. A gentle aesthete, a brilliant teacher and the best man at our wedding.

At his church funeral, men in black suits descended like crows onto a coffin formal and solid as oak but boring as a Victorian bookend. Where was Mick? He, the anarchist dreamer who once ate the Christmas decorations in a country pub. What did his funeral celebration have to do with life, or art or us or his family or anything life- (or even death-) enhancing. The over-riding mood from the cavernous church of his final ceremony was of sinister blackness. Towards the end of his life he had meditated and painted garden flowers till they looked like luminous planets. This ceremony was everything he was not. Why couldn't he be buried like that ancient ploughman in a running position, pushing his plough? Be sheltered in a circle of old hog's hair paintbrushes in a sprinkling of the red ochre powder used by other cultures, to symbolise the blood of the earth? Where was the poetry?

Rosamund

Then another friend, a wild comic actress, kills herself. Immediately, her family decide that the best place for the funeral and memorial ceremony is inside a church.

I guess she would have preferred a dramatic landscape lit by fireworks. But it is hard under terrible circumstances to think clearly, let alone invent new forms of ritual or find relevant environments.

As the funeral was a purely family affair three hundred miles away, we designed a small separate ceremony. This was mainly for our own grounding but hopefully a sympathetic offering to the relatives in their extreme pain. Living in Ulverston on the edge of the Lake District in the North West of England the location was our nearby seashore. The following poem sent to the relatives before the actual funeral, describes our action:

Where you had both walked
in that desert of Morecambe Bay
we placed a circle of five cream roses.
Then upon the rippled sand
we spelled your name
with the tiniest of pink and white shells.
Finally we made a lantern.
Inside its crude shelter
of deep yellow paper
an oasis of more shells
surround a fat candle.
Outside, a gentle cairn.
Sticks and stones,
mellowing leaves of rowan and beech,
one tattered gull's feather
and one perfect red berry -
which fell at random.
The oiled circle, on the crumpled paper,
ran to earth to become
a mountain of tears.
We left.
Leaving the candle to the West Wind
and the roses to the evening tide.
Out in that bare expanse of cold sand we also tried
to sing, a blessing from a mutual show of ten years
before.
I am your guardian angel.
Spirit of the planet.
I will gently guide you through
the cracks of blackened earth.
I will guide you through the darkness.
Beyond the nightmare.
To the cave, the cave of distant hope.

At the strong memorial service for Rosamund, in the Actors'
Church, colleagues read poems and stories or sang songs
connected with her theatrical life (even playing "I'm forever
blowing bubbles" on her musical saw). To follow this we
organised a final gathering in an oval-shaped dance hall near
the church. The space was decorated with white bunting and
paper cuts; a table was covered in memorabilia, snapshots
and letters; a poster-size photograph of Rosamund smiling
was fastened to a wall in the centre under the mirror ball; a
boat-shaped moon of a lantern made of white tissue paper was
carefully illuminated with one candle. To the tunes of a small

accordion ceilidh band we danced round this focus, told more stories and poems and helped some children, including her son, to perform a small play. Coming after the more formal church service, here was an opportunity for release and even catharsis.

Jan

Jan died unexpectedly in January.

> "You're always welcome here" were the last words you said to me. That was last spring I think. Then, within the winding of winter, you died. And tomorrow on the final quarter of a February moon it's your cremation. My sadness after just two breakfast conversations, is a frail shell in the ocean of fathomless bereavement. What may I offer to your husband and family?"

> I saw
> a photograph of you
> singing inwardly in a Cornish wind.
> I saw
> a well-spring of sparkling wine
> bearing an ancient tuning fork.
> I saw
> a passionate nurturing of your children.
> Where love became a sacrifice of love.
> And I was welcomed
> with cocoa and snap crackle cornflakes.
> My frail shell was given a safe harbour.
> May you be welcomed so on your continuing voyage.

This Christian funeral in St Michael and All Angels Church, Bedford Park, London was excellent. Mainly because it was brilliantly organised by her husband John, an experienced theatre producer. The church setting was beautiful, the sermon particular, John's oration amazingly cool, and moving, and St Paul's Girls' School madrigal choir exceptional.

The only thing that hadn't crossed John's mind was the crematorium in Mortlake. Fortunately it was better than most, and in the five spare minutes before the next cremation

I was able to contribute a small decoration. I had made four paper cuts (one for each of her daughters), and "Blu-tacked" these to the wall lights. Cut with a scalpel from white A4 typing paper, they depicted a small boat voyaging on the sea, its tree-mast sails turning back to leaves (see images on back cover). We also placed a cardboard painted lantern at the foot of the coffin.

Unfortunately no-one had mentioned a crematorium organist. So at the end of the service there was an embarrassed silence. The vicar waved a cue-ing finger discreetly behind his surplice. Still silence. Without a briefing, the organist didn't know what to do. The vicar's finger became more animated. Still silence. Then as we left and the pews emptied, the organ suddenly struck up with an arbitrary hymn which no-one can recall.

Later John wrote:

> "After the service we stuck the paper cuts on a west-facing window at home. That was good; they stayed there for six months."

> "... My main point would be that in the time allowed by the average death, I didn't have space or energy to engineer a proper rite of passage. Indeed I am not certain if I would have been the right person. The service was an adrenaline-driven improvisation and not everyone has a superb meaningful group (or its personal equivalent) to hand. Lots of food for thought."

Nearly two years later (at Hallowe'en and All Souls Day) he sent us an autumn present, a white envelope of toasted pumpkin seeds, and wrote:

> Two harvests since she died
> And I still toast
> Pumpkin seeds from
> Grinning Jack O'Lantern
> Uncertain business
> Crisping the kernels
> Shrouded in the husk
> Sweetness or cinders?
> No-one knows
> Until the seed is cracked.

Memorial Services

It is easier to create a ceremony for a memorial event than for a funeral because there is more time to plan.

Howard

Howard's memorial service followed rather quickly, in weeks rather than months, after the cremation service. Although not an overt Christian, he requested his ashes be buried in a local churchyard overlooking Morecambe Bay. Friends organised the many aspects. A long walk to and from the remote rural church was proposed and a clear guide map drawn, a new composition for two voices, accordion and guitar was performed in the church, a specially painted casket was first displayed on a plinth in the centre of the aisle and subsequently buried in a neat hole in the churchyard and covered with a flat slate inscribed with cut letters.

Everyone contributed using their appropriate skills. At the final afternoon and evening party, souvenir photographs were displayed, stories told, music performed, toasts drunk and a final full stop created with a runway of silver rain fireworks leading to one extraordinary climactic burst of silver rain rocketed five hundred feet into the evening sky.

My role was to paint the casket. After the cremation, the ashes were delivered from the undertaker in a shiny wooden box, varnished on the top and the sides. These are work-a-day reliquaries of Victorian ancestry, inoffensive if a little pompous. The price varies, but they should be about £30.00 off the undertaker's shelf.

I unscrewed both the engraved chromium plate from the top of the box then the bottom of the box itself. After carefully depositing the dusty ashes in a separate container (there is about a couple of kilos of them), I removed the varnish with varnish stripper and scraper. It would have been easier of course to have ordered an unfinished box from the manufacturer but someone else bought it. After washing and drying, I filled any slight cracks with wood filler then painted it with white wood primer and undercoat as necessary.

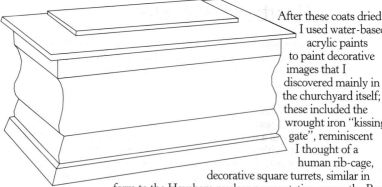

Standard oak casket for cremated remains.

After these coats dried I used water-based acrylic paints to paint decorative images that I discovered mainly in the churchyard itself; these included the wrought iron "kissing gate", reminiscent I thought of a human rib-cage, decorative square turrets, similar in form to the Heysham nuclear power station across the Bay, a November 5th bonfire waiting to be lit on the beach, and people carrying simple lanterns and a ladder. The symbols reflected Howard's work, which had been the management of celebratory theatrical events. The colours were deep and resonant. Pinks and reds echoing through an infinite night sky of black cobalt and ultramarine blue. I added subtle coats of fluorescent magenta enamel varnish until the casket burned with a jewelled fairground glow. It was the best I could do for Howard.

After carefully pouring the ashes back into the upside down casket (ensuring there was paper to cover the table as it's easy to scatter the ash), putting a secret poem inside and rescrewing the base, I gave the box a final varnish and returned the chromium plaque. On its plinth in the church it looked well; more representative of Howard's colourful life I thought than the dull, if respectable, light oak of the original container. I hope he would have approved. Maybe the puritan in him would have preferred a deadpan wood grain – I should have asked him while he was alive. As far as I know he had never been to Church in the ten years I knew him. However, his suddenly acquired priest remarked that the box was bright and appropriate (and different!), and made with love and care ... Howard would have chuckled.

The design for Howard's casket.

As he would have at his funeral service in the crematorium a few weeks before when a friend placed his new panama straw hat and a copy of that morning's *Guardian* on his coffin lid. He always read *The Guardian* before going to work. Today was no different except on this morning the paper contained his own obituary!

The Dead Good Funerals Book

Football Supporter

After painting Howard's casket and after reading that many football fans in Glasgow want their ashes to be scattered on the pitch, I created another casket for an (imagined) football supporter.

The technique of painting is the same as for Howard's casket. In this case though, the pictures are based on football. The image of a football kicked high into the stratosphere and goal posts without nets so that a ball (or soul? or spirit?) might not be constrained. One side of the casket depicts a full stadium. The other side an empty ground with a vast lettered scarf spelling out "Goodbye Harry". Underneath are football studs, a surreal joke I couldn't resist.

Casket for the ashes of an (imagined) football fan, designed by John Fox.

So many football fans want their ashes to be scattered on

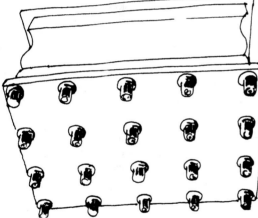

the pitches these days that groundsmen resist. Maybe a casket painted in club colours would be some compensation? In Carlisle a cardboard coffin was painted in the colours of Carlisle United.

In both Howard's case and that of the invented footballer's casket, the source of the poetry was found in the location of their lives.

Finally, a diary note:

Lismore, New South Wales, Australia. 17 December 1991

"We create a funeral ceremony for an Australian friend, Jyllie, whose father has just died in England. In the garden and house we decorate spaces with strings of white paper cutouts using salmon and moon imagery. (Her father had been an amateur fisherman.) In a sheltered corner by a tree there is a place for meditation, with a table of family snapshots. Sue makes a small sculptural fire a metre high – a dumpy tower constructed with circles of chunky wood. I make a ceremonial lantern with white tissue paper and willow sticks which I construct as a miniature replica of her father's garden shed. Inside this Jyllie places the last photograph of herself with her father. In the evening, after reading from Rilke, Jyllie places the lantern on the fire. The solemn atmosphere is counterbalanced by her friend playing Glenn Miller on a small electric keyboard in a far corner of the garden.

I also write a poem for her based on memories of her complex relationship with her father. It ends: ... "the real bridge is love, where you met as two grown-ups."

Rilke also wrote:

Once, ritual lament would have been chanted: women would have been paid to beat their breasts and howl for you all night, when all is silent. Where can we find such customs now? So many have long since disappeared or been disowned. That's what you have come for; to retrieve the laments that were omitted. Can you hear me? I would like to fling my voice out like a cloth over the fragments of your death, and keep pulling at it until it is torn to pieces, and all my words would have to walk around shivering, in the tatters of that voice; if lament were enough.

First Encounters with Death

A couple of weeks before her twenty-first birthday my stepsister died of tuberculosis. I was seven. I remember saying goodbye to her as she lay in bed. I wasn't allowed to go close in case I got infected so I waved farewell from the bedroom doorway until I was whisked away by my auntie in a bus with a big round chromium radiator. I sat next to the window in the front right-hand seat. When I was brought back to the house a week or so later Jean was

dead and buried. Having been brought up by my mother as a
Roman Catholic I was taught that all I had to do was pray and
everything would be alright. I knew Jesus worked miracles. So
every night for a year (in the tent I made in bed) I cried and
prayed for Jean to come back. After a year I realized grown
ups and priests tell lies.

My next encounter with death was during National Service
with the Royal West African Frontier Force in Ghana when I
was 19. As a naive first lieutenant on an orderly officer's duty
round I had to check out "a body in the latrine sir!" It was
a stillbirth. I arranged for it to be buried in an ammunition
box in the flower bed of the medical centre. That year they
grew wonderful geraniums and thereafter I arranged for more
ammunition boxes to be delivered to more dead children.
Infant mortality was high and it offended my English and
Catholic taste to imagine that babies' bodies would be buried
or disappear without even a makeshift coffin.

I find it hard to think about death. Most people I know don't
dwell on it. It's not in our biological make up. An old friend,
Peter, told me for the first time last week, that when he was
coming home from the shipyard once, aged 19, a man next
to him on the bus had a fatal heart attack. Twenty years later
Peter still wakes up with panic attacks.

Despite the hundreds of media images we see of fantasy and
news video violence few of us in the west ever see a dead
body. The first proper body I saw was my mother in her
coffin. I was disturbed by her yellow waxen face and her
suddenly acquired moustache. A few years later my father's
corpse was the next I saw. This time I was more prepared and
even took some photographs of him in his coffin.

Even so it was a shock. Though I had seen him in hospital
recently and thought I was composed I was still amazed that
such a big man could shrink to become so small and bird-like,
with hollow cheeks and hooked nose beak.

In both cases there was only the slightest connection between
the living person and the dead body. The late Barry Long,
spiritual teacher, has produced a number of books and a tape
about death and dying. I found these helpful.

Barry Long's viewpoint is very considered and although I am

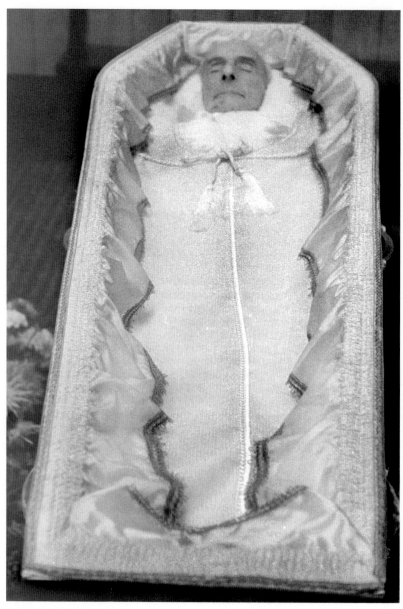

My father in his coffin.

reluctant to quote him out of context, his thoughts are useful. He led me to understand that facing up to death can be a profound catalyst for personal transformation.

In Barry's own words:

> "There is an art to dying. When death comes it is always today."

> "Death is the most important thing in your life."

> "Death is the world's best kept secret. Every day thousands of people die in the UK" (mostly in bed in hospital - Ed.) "yet all we see is an occasional hearse carrying a box laden with flowers."

> "Death is a dead body."

> "We human beings in our modern society are no longer simple where death is concerned. We can't see it as it is anymore, can't look at it objectively. We've handed death over, all the dead bodies, for others to deal with. To officialdom.
> We've opted out. In much older societies where people handled their dead and buried their dead, they didn't fear death. By having it around them everyday they were reminded of the simple truth that death is just a dead body. They didn't need to speculate as we do. It was there in front of them. When you are in touch with death you don't fear it. You don't fear anything you are in touch with."

> "If we face up to death before it happens it would be ... an ennobling experience for all concerned."

We have to be wary of a cabal of professionals, medical practitioners, undertakers, and local council officials who can seem to exclude us, so that we feel we are voyeuristic ghouls if we show any interest in dead bodies. This is not necessarily a plot of course, rather a mixture of well-meaningness, overwork, poor training and so on, but it is symptomatic of our commodity culture that our personal responsibilities are often undermined. We need to be vigilant. Death *is* secret.

Unless someone in the corner shop or on a bus next to us has a cardiac arrest, or unless we are involved in a traffic accident or a war it is unlikely that we will witness death at first hand.

In his **The Lives of a Cell** (1974) the biologist Lewis Thomas wrote a stimulating short essay called "Death in the Open" giving a different perspective.

> "Everything in the world dies, but we only know about it as a kind of abstraction. If you stand in a meadow, at the edge of a hillside, and look around carefully, almost everything you catch sight of is in the process of dying, and most things will be dead long before you are. If it were not for the constant renewal and replacement going on before your eyes, the whole place would turn to stone and sand under your feet."

He tells us that there are 25 million insects hanging in the air over every temperate square mile, all steadily dying. He asks how often do we see a dead bird compared with the thousands we see on the wing, and mentions "how animals seem to have an instinct for perfoming death alone, hidden". He has seen many squirrels in his garden but never a dead one.

> "I suppose it is just as well. If the earth were otherwise, and all the dying were done in the open, with the dead there to be looked at, we would never have it out of our minds. We can forget about it much of the time, or think of it as an accident to be avoided, somehow. But it does make the process of dying seem more exceptional than it really is, and harder to engage in at the times when we must ourselves engage."

Three billion of us on the earth will die within this lifetime. fifty million a year. Most of us will disappear back into the earth without so much as a wink at the others and, well before the middle of the 21st century, our replacements will total over 12 billion.

> "It is hard to see how we can continue to keep the secret, with such multitudes doing the dying. We will have to give up the notion that death is catastrophe, or detestable, or avoidable or even

> strange. We will need to learn more about the
> cycling of life in the rest of the system, and about
> our connection to the process. Everything that
> comes alive seems to be in the trade for something
> that dies, cell for cell. There might be some comfort
> in the recognition of synchrony, in the formation
> that we all go down together, in the best of
> company."

If death is secret either because it is, or because there is a conspiracy or because we just prefer not to notice, it's not going to go away.

In one of George Herriman's timeless comic strips Krazy Kat asks Mr Bee:

> "Do you think, Mr Bee, that what happened
> yesterday will happen again?"
> "It most certainly will Krazy. History, events,
> accidents, thoughts, jokes, you, I, everything and
> nothing must repeat itself. Everything is just nothing
> repeating itself. Ashes to ashes is the best repeating
> act we do ... so don't worry it will happen."

Other cultures have made more intensive studies of the psychological, practical and spiritual processes of dying and death than we have in the West. **The Tibetan Book of Living and Dying** by Sogyal Rinpoche for example gives a good overview. The stages of dying can be long and complex. Letting go of life is an art to be studied, and placed on the National Curriculum!

The North Central Florida Hospice has produced an article entitled **Preparing for Approaching Death** which contains a detailed description of the final stages of dying, designed to inform family, friends and carers and those facing death. It is available for free download via the World Wide Web.

From our own culture I found the following in the Rev J N Faux's **Church Folklore** (Griffith Farran & Co, London, 1894):

> "... not a few medical men of wide experience
> entertain a strong conviction that the departure of
> the soul from the body is a much more protracted

operation than is commonly supposed; and some I know, are of the opinion that the mental faculties of the patient, under ordinary circumstance, become keener as the end approaches. It is quite possible that this may be the case, and such possibility should always be remembered by those who are in attendance upon the dying, so that silence may be maintained for some minutes at least, and outward expressions of sorrow kept in check, even when the spirit has apparently taken flight. Of course I do not mean that any prayers that are being said at the moment of the seeming departure should cease – far from it. The very fact of the devotions being continued may, for all we know, be of unspeakable comfort to the departing soul."

Understanding the nature of dying and the way that it is usually handled in our culture is fundamental because the form and style of funeral ceremonies are, overtly or implicitly, informed by attitudes and prejudices. If we decide that established methods or belief systems are irrelevant to us then we must signal the alternative or the usual practices will prevail.

Somewhere in the night a mollusc is growing
- but where does he get his flesh from?
- he grows with the little pale balls
in the pits of childish stomachs:
these knots that inflate in the belly
and beneath the rib cage,
that people call "fear of death".

Rene Daumal (1908 - 1944) wrote this early poem recalling his experience as a six year old child. Throughout his life he sought to conquer such fear.

Reclaiming the Agenda

Although this book is a nuts and bolts manual for funerals, rather than a tract, the wider picture cannot be ignored. Values underlie the rites of passage ceremonies we choose, or accept, so we should examine the basis of our dominant culture, which sends out such mixed messages about death and dying.

1   We live in a consumer society where it is morally acceptable for some to make a lucrative profit. This can mean that we are persuaded to spend too much to make a funeral (or a wedding) significant. Our guilt and wish to give generously are exploited and the event is measured by cost rather than meaning. In our capitalist system, driven as it is by market profits, it doesn't pay to acknowledge death. Would we continue to shop 'til we drop if we knew the day and hour of our death? Would we exploit developing countries if we understood that their life expectancy was half that of ours and would we tolerate so easily death from cars, alcohol, drugs, tobacco and pollution if we understood the link between manufacturing, advertising and collecting taxes?

2   We live in a war economy where killing other human beings is an acceptable way of resolving conflict. Britain is the world's second biggest exporter of weapons. Many of our industries, jobs and our national economy depend on this trade. We have a vested interest in peddling death. A combative and competitive way of thinking, with its simplistic Anglo-Saxon dualism of Good versus Evil, is so embedded in our culture, that we take for granted the huge number of gratuitous and violent pretend killings we see on TV, at the movies, or in children's play and video games. Brutalised by such propaganda we become uncritical. The inconsequential death of an individual or a whole alien group is trivialised and the real pain and mystery of death is ignored or fantasised.

3   We live in a scientific age. It is possible to imagine that one day we could live for hundreds of years. But would we want to? If death and recycling are a natural part of our existence then would it perhaps be better to apply more resources to understanding the process, rather than spending billions via the lucrative health industry* on offsetting the inevitable? Answering this of course, especially in a global context, throws up provocative moral and ethical dilemmas for us all. It also raises the serious question of euthanasia.(*For a shocking assessment of the marketing tactics of multi-national drug companies see New Internationalist 362 – November 2003, www.newint.org).

AFTER APPLE-PICKING

Robert Frost

My long two-pointed ladder's sticking through a tree
Toward heaven still.
And there's a barrel that I didn't fill
Beside it, and there may be two or three
Apples I didn't pick upon some bough.
But I am done with apple-picking now.
Essence of winter sleep is on the night,
The scent of apples; I am drowsing off.
I cannot shake the shimmer from my sight
I got from looking through a pane of glass
I skimmed this morning from the water-trough,
And held against the world of hoary grass.
It melted, and I let it fall and break.

But I was well
Upon my way to sleep before it fell,
And I could tell
What form my dreaming was about to take.
Magnified apples appear and reappear,
Stem end and blossom end,
And every fleck of russet showing clear.
My instep arch not only keeps the ache,
It keeps the pressure of a ladder-round.
And I keep hearing from the cellar-bin
That rumbling sound
Of load on load of apples coming in.

For I have had too much
Of apple-picking; I am overtired
Of the great harvest I myself desired.
There were ten thousand thousand fruit to touch,
Cherish in hand, lift down, and not let fall,
For all
That struck the earth,
No matter if not bruised, or spiked with stubble,
Went surely to the cider-apple heap
As of no worth.
One can see what will trouble
This sleep of mine, whatever sleep it is.
Were he not gone,
The woodchuck could say whether it's like his
Long sleep, as I describe its coming on,
Or just some human sleep.

Rites of Passage

"Rites of passage mark the transition from one situation to another and from one cosmic or social world order to another."

Arnold Van Gennep, **Les Rites de Passage** (1909)

"Rites of passage are a category of rituals that mark the passage of an individual through the life cycle, from one stage to another over time, from one role or social position to the next, integrating the human and cultural experiences with biological destiny; birth, reproduction and death."

Barbara Myerhoff, **Celebration** (1982)

The image of a journey can be helpful. We are always moving from the past to the future. Nothing stands still. The planet turns, it gets dark and we get older. If we try to return to old haunts they seem different because we have changed. Everything is in flux, including us.

But equally, on journeys, we are all familiar with gateways, turnstiles and barbed wire or even obligatory viewing points. Also the shape and size of gateways can vary according to whether they are public or private, for a group or an individual. Rites of passage arise quite naturally but they are often also culturally imposed.

A "teenager" may be a convenient customer or client targeted in the market economy, rather than a human being at a certain stage of biological development, but the dominant capitalist structure is challenged when those teenagers steal cars for joy-riding, tag or scratch windows in shopping malls or tattoo themselves. In reaction to the status quo and in the absence of any adequate rites prescribed by the elders, they are consciously or unconsciously inventing. Also definitions of "old" are changing, not just because we live longer but because, as the average age of the population increases in Western Europe there is money and power in the grey tide. What should signify "old"? Is it redundancy, retirement, rail card, bus pass, loss of teeth, entry to an old folks' home, failure to get on **Blind Date**, senility or the destitution we suffer because we failed to make provision for a pension?

The Dead Good Funerals Book

If rites of passage are for both the individual *and* the community and wider society, how do we stop the oppression of outmoded values and achieve the right balance particularly when the "individual" is irrational (such as love-crazed couples; over-indulgent parents; a baby; a corpse; or a person with an advanced degenerative disease)? If the intelligent parents of intelligent young couples are persuaded to spend thousands of pounds on a white wedding (when the majority of relationships break up) who really gains from such reinforcement of pair bonding? The couple; or the fashion magazines and the vast wedding industry?

Our rich multi-cultural society is changing rapidly. New value systems are emerging which will underpin new rites. Many find life incomprehensible and the daily grind difficult, so at a time of uncertainty, if the established channels don't work, there is a need for innovative alternatives. At moments of stress we need well-designed procedures which bring people together, that comfort the vulnerable and offer a supportive framework for affirming the special points in one's life. Some, such rites of passage as the initiations of joy-riding, evolve naturally but some may need to be invented.

Rites of Passage present us with the contradictions of our nature and by acting them out symbolically through a sensual and physical, rather than an intellectual process, we learn and pass on what it is to be human. With the vastness of this new millennium before us, we need all the help we can get.

Inappropriate ceremonies can be worse than no ceremonies at all. We need clear new rites to ground us. Anyone who has experienced the desolation at the funeral of someone we love conducted by strangers, devoid of personal significance with no power to help us celebrate the deceased and mourn our loss, should take no convincing. People who become isolated and resort to illness or breakdown or psychiatrists could use ceremonies of integration to help them cope with conflict or complexity. Those retiring, leaving home, stopping work (either through choice or redundancy), changing jobs, changing status, reaching fifty, moving or building a house, divorcing, as well as in the traditional areas of birth, baptism, coming of age, marrying or dying could benefit from considered declarations of position with a sympathetic group.

The question for a fragmented and rootless secular society is not whether we need rites of passage ceremonies or not, but rather what form they should take, who provides them, are they private or public, what are they celebrating and who are the celebrants? Should they be trained, and if so by whom?

The form of a rite of passage

The basic forms are similar in different cultures and centuries and perhaps more surprisingly are also similar for varied occasions. The underlying structure of a funeral ceremony need not, for example, be very different from that of a wedding.

Nearly eighty years ago Gennep spotted a universal three-part structure, a logical sequence of:

separation ... transition ... re-incorporation

to take a person from an old position via an interval to a new status.

Another way of putting it is:

extinguish ... pause to adjust ... create the new

After change we are integrated with a new status and ideally greater wisdom. According to your choice of religion this applies both to the living and the dead. The difficult transition of the bereaved is that they have "to disentangle themselves not only from the past but also from the previously envisaged future."

Such sequences can work in real space and time, within a self-contained invented world and quite mysteriously and cleverly, in both at once.

I am writing this in a 16th century tenement in Nice. Within a five-minute walk from our bedsitter are four large baroque Roman Catholic churches. Although their heavy bells ring throughout the night they have mostly been shut and empty. Empty, that is, except for the cathedral which has been open on Sundays, also for a Monday morning funeral – for a murdered policeman, a Friday wedding and for Christmas Mass.

On this occasion, however, the cathedral is filled with over a thousand spectators. A large percentage are a worshipping congregation, but many, including us, are clearly occasional visitors, attending because of a traditional need to be together with others on the special occasion of a Christmas Midnight.

And special it is; a site-specific art work, with a small orchestra and choir performing well-known carols and Bach fragments beneath jewelled domes, elegant candelabra and statues as gold (and nearly as rude) as those in many an Edwardian theatre.

The five male priests and the clutch of altar boys are as dull and incommunicative as the tacky loudspeakers but no matter. Around the winter solstice time all humans, in the Northern Hemisphere at least, have an ancient need to cling together in warm shelter in the hope that the disappeared sun will return. The Celts, the Pagans, the Christians wished a light would appear in the dark forest and, whatever the precise symbolism or mythology of each religion, we all ensure it happens, year after year.

And so it was in France. I was pleased that St Francis of Assisi invented the crib with convenient domestic animals (including on this occasion vast polystyrene rocks, a minute Shetland pony and a disconsolate Jersey cow) because a thousand candles could be lit. Light did come in the darkness and though I am not a Christian believer I could sing raucously, with my Turkish neighbour, "Once in Royal David's City". He sang in French and I sang in English to celebrate, yet again, the luminous timewarp of a Jewish star-baby descending before the crucified edifice of his mature self on a marble altar.

In this Christian event there is a complicated pattern of public and private social activity unfolding within the structure of a set of beliefs or sacred knowledge. Here a mixed congregation is sharing a theoretical belief in a God in human form and worshipping that God through the practice of hymns and prayers and an agreed iconography or symbolic code.

Gennep's three part sequence is obvious. We left the secular market place via the Cathedral threshold to enter a symbolically decorated environment. Here through prayers, music, traditional stories and a beautifully contrived candle-lit atmosphere, we were put in the mood for reaching a sacred deity in the company of a community with shared beliefs.

In terms of overall Christian symbolism there is also a three part structure in the story. After his life on earth Jesus is crucified, resurrects and returns. Now nearly two thousand years later via "transubstantiation", a willing congregation still "miraculously" shares his eternal flesh through an infinity of communion wafers.

On Christmas night, in the middle of winter, the cycle is neatly compressed and theatrically demonstrated. Directly under a plaster replica of himself nailed to a bloody wooden cross he is reborn, as a spanking fresh babe with a heavenly star, evergreens, farm animals and a joyous font of virgin's milk.

Separation, transition and reincorporation depicted on multiple macro and micro levels in clear down to earth pictures inviting participation. A good lesson.

An archetype. Try also compost, seed, blossom, fruit, feast, shit, bust and back again. Or any winter to summer cosmology with trees, spilled fertilising blood and new growth. Some people find such metaphors useful when visualising the structure of a ritual. Eggs, birds and flight. Boats and voyages with attendant storms and harbours are other handy transformation sequences.

In case all of these seem a bit "wholemealy" there is always Meatloaf's mini-opera with the song "Objects in the rear-view mirror". Here we see that "The soul is a car travelling on the highway of life". It is tempting to rewrite old mythologies in modern imagery. Motorways, parking lots and spaghetti junctions controlled by the Holy Ghost, with red, amber and green halos ... St Paul handing out parking fines payable to the Jehovah District Council ...

To summarise: complex poetry can flow round a simple armature, and the stronger the armature the more we can wrap round it. This "symbolic template" is enlivened with permanent or temporary architecture, images, music, dance, incense and mythological stories etc. So we transport ourselves through dreaming, or trance or prayer from the mundane to the sacred or "less ordinary" or heightened reality and celebrate within the support of a temporary community or congregation which shares common rules and beliefs. This exuberant process reinforces our identity and our humanity, ideally recharging our vitality, and gives us a sense of direction before we return to being alone with the everyday.

Rites of passage are wrapped in ritual and may logically be enacted *with or without religion.*

Why Religion?

You can be born, named, married, divorced, made redundant and lose all your teeth without the involvement of a religious institution, but at death the Church hones in. Usually a religion or a set of beliefs does inform most rites of passage. When people complain that a funeral service felt irrelevant to them or even insulting to the deceased it is often because either the service was too impersonal or the majority of the congregation didn't share the beliefs or form of worship of that religion, or the priest hijacked the occasion to preach impersonal propaganda.

For many of us in Britain, Christianity is still our cultural norm and it's hard to consider anything else ... but as there are at least six major religions and hundreds of others to choose from, there *are* alternatives. Once we know what we believe in or more importantly what we don't believe in, it's easier to consider an appropriate ceremony for ourself or our relations, to mark the end of our time.

Even attending a Christian funeral ceremony (in a culture where that faith has been institutionalised and artificially maintained through the state with our monarchy, schools and the BBC etc.) can be like entering a foreign land. We feel embarrassed because we don't understand the concepts, customs and language. Christian culture is still so dominant that most funerals, even those in supposedly neutral crematoria, end up as Christian or pseudo-Christian. Now that relatively few people are practising Christians this is frustrating for clergy and congregation alike, and it is time to set up new and maybe secular spaces where the right ceremonies may be easily practised.

We may share a set of beliefs and accept a given liturgy but the physical and aesthetic qualities of existing church ceremonies can still often be improved. Items to look at are: live music, the placing of the congregation, the focus of the architecture and lighting, the style of the coffin, the nature of flower and other decorations, the relevance of the sermon (which often depends on the priest's research), the particularness of prayers and poetry and the standard of printed written leaflets and books. The best funerals are those where belief and aesthetics work together; are shared by celebrant, undertaker, deceased and congregation; and where strangers are made to feel welcome.

It is not surprising in a multi-cultural and multi-aged society with many tastes and changing traditions that it's rare to experience unanimity about the quality of a "good" funeral. Even when everything goes well the occasion is always unnerving and we often transfer our fear (and anger) to the undertaker, officiant or family. In the face of death, finding scapegoats is a natural way of dealing with insecurity. Equally, our anxiety can be manipulated by priests, undertakers and relations. Once people paid a tramp to eat bread off the corpse in order to expurgate sin but now we find other channels to hand over to convenient professionals. They can provide a perfect service and work hard in unpleasant and difficult circumstances but it's worth considering what we may lose for ourselves by giving responsibility to outside experts.

Religion provides comfort for millions but it can become an addiction. Addictions stop us taking responsibility for ourselves and dependence makes us open to exploitation. Also as religion soon gets entangled with politics, wars may be triggered through religious extremism and fundamentalism often driven by fanatical priesthoods of authoritarian, celibate men. So it's at least worth asking whether, in view of the harm that is done in its name, we would be better off without any religions at all.

Towards a Definition of Religion

Religion is difficult to define. Victor Turner the anthropologist suggested somewhat tautologically:

"strict observance of ceremonies, moral scruples, conscientiousness, an object of worship, a holy

thing or place, the worship of a particular deity and
a bond between man and the gods."

Derived from the latin word "religio" the root is eurocentric
and it doesn't explain much unless we know what concepts
like "holy", "deity", "gods", "worship" and "moral" mean.

If any twelve people gathering together agree to believe in
something and evolve a coherent and public and systematic
demonstration of that belief (which might include prayers
to and meditation on the object of their choice) then you
have a religion. If a deity or an intangible being or a superior
invisible force is needed they could substitute Nature, or
Chance, or The Planet Earth, or Timelessness, or Creativity,
or The Great Unknown, or the Big Salmon, Mammon, or
Consumerism. No one could prove that this group of twelve
were without a religion or even a god.

The **Larousse Dictionary of Beliefs and Religions** states
that:

> "No single definition will suffice to encompass the
> varied sets of traditions practices and ideas which
> constitute different religions. Some religions involve
> the belief in and worship of a god or gods but this
> is not true of all. Christianity, Islam,and Judaism
> are theistic religions, while Buddhism does not
> require a belief in gods, and where it does occur,
> the gods are not considered important. There are
> theories of religion which construe it as wholly a
> human phenomenon, without any supernatural or
> transcendent origin and point of reference, while
> others argue that some such reference is the essence
> of the matter. Several other viewpoints exist and
> there are often boundary disputes regarding the
> application of the concept. For example debate
> continues as to whether Confucianism is properly
> to be considered a religion; and some writers argue
> that Marxism is, in important respects, a religion."

"Belief" is subjective and hard to verify objectively. You
either have "faith" and "believe" or you don't. You either
acknowledge "divine powers" or "divine beings" or maybe
intuit "invisible and intangible and superior forces" or you
don't. All religions claim to have the truest insight so you

might prefer to make up your own. Intuition is an exceptional guru.

The Function of a Funeral

- Disposal of the body

- Treatment of the spirit

- Concern for the bereaved

In carrying out these functions funeral rites are as rich as humanity; the main teachings of all faiths find their meaning at death and it's usually our religious beliefs that affect the way the dead are treated and how they are remembered.

As there are hundreds of ways of worshipping there are equally hundreds of conceivable funeral rites. Fashions change, sometimes rapidly.

When worshipping we can sing, dance, pray, meditate, parade, play music, make and decorate spaces inside or outside, eat, fast, make a noise or be silent, be extravagant or austere, all in a group or on our own. Mourning can be short or very long and the bereaved may suffer, or enjoy many kinds of status change. Funerary artefacts may be very simple or extraordinarily complex. Very inventive or dull and pompous.

It helps to know whether we expect or want to be reborn (in the same or different form); whether we have souls that can separate from our bodies; whether these souls have any level of human consciousness and whether they hang about, reappear on special or difficult occasions or really disappear for ever.

Many people believe that the physical and spiritual aspects of a person are separate and that death may be the moment of judgement. After death the spirit or soul may go to a different world, sometimes helped by go-betweens such as angels or spirit guardians, and either re-join the body or take a different form. The soul may be sent or venture to heaven or hell, to suffer or mature or await return to life in a better or worse form from the ancestral garage.

Following the pattern of: body disposal, concern for the spirit and respect for the mourners, there are key differences. For example Christianity, Judaism and Islam stress that human life is once and for all, so the physical container of that life ... the body ... is crucial; whereas in the reincarnation faiths of Buddhism, Hinduism and Sikhism, the physical shell which has housed the karma (or soul) is seen to be less significant.

A subjective look at Christian funeral rites

Christianity is ambiguous about the end of life. On the one hand there is the belief that death is not an end and we will see each other again in heaven, or in hell if we fail the Final Judgement Day test. (Whether it's reconstituted bodies plus souls that go on to eternity or just souls is a matter of opinion amongst Christian theologians.) But, whatever the form we are re-assembled in, the Church equally recognizes that a particular life on earth has come to an end. Consequently in Christianity there is great concern for the sense of loss of the mourners in addition to gaining the rewards of eternal life.

More so than in some other religions the dead body is treated with great respect. In many Christian funeral services the priest dressed in black meets the coffin outside and then precedes it into the Church along with pall-bearers and chief mourners.

Life after death is emphasised at the beginning and the whole service is constructed around resurrection symbolised by Christ rising from the Tomb.

"I am the Resurrection and the Life says the Lord"

The words: "Earth to earth, ashes to ashes, dust to dust" are often used at the graveside, even when the body has not been cremated and there is little chance of ash or dust. But this singular, wondrous and even pagan poetry reflects the belief that we were created from the Earth to await the Final Day.

Until the last century, of course, all Christians were buried on the understanding that it would be easier to keep the accounts if we had a constant parking plot. But land gets more expensive, bodies accumulate and not surprisingly fashions change, as they usually do under economic pressure. So now in many Christian countries cremation is three times as popular as burial and the ashes are buried or scattered often in consecrated ground so the ancient poetry comes well into its own once again.

Throughout Christian burial and other services, the mercy of God is continually beseeched that people are alleged to be full of guilt and sin and can never be worthy of or as good as the Father, Son and the Holy Ghost (who is a bit mysterious and less popular these days). So penitents pray for forgiveness, for themselves and for the dead, mainly to Our Father, a bit to Jesus and (in relatively modern times as these things go) to Jesus's mum as well, hoping that our soul and the souls of our friends will stay pure enough long enough to join an extremely mighty herd of good people who are fortunate to be saved for ever from the evil kingdom of Satan.

If you are a believer it is hard to beat a good Christian service with its rousing but usually old fashioned hymns and prayers, a sensitive audible priest, a tuneful choir, an attentive organist, and soaring architecture. Undoubtedly when they are suffering the shock of bereavement it offers immense comfort and release – for mourners are able to express their distress with solid community support. A big Requiem Mass can be an awe-inspiring spectacle. For Pope or humble minion believer alike an after-life is good security and, in most cases, it is a joyous thought that one day we will meet up with our loved ones again. If you believe, it works.

The circular wreath containing the emptiness of eternity is a perfect symbol. Today though the expensively perfect flowers often grown in chemically polluted third world hothouses are piled excessively on the coffin or on the ground in cellophane packets. Black is traditional but in excess a relatively new tradition invented by Queen Victoria. The black pall on the coffin symbolises the eternal darkness of the tomb from which Jesus and his followers can rise in a halo (or illuminated wreath) of incandescent and healing light.

The World's other Major Faiths and their Funeral Customs

This book is no comprehensive guide to comparative religion but it's instructive to see how varied funeral customs can be and how much of what we take for granted is conditioned by culture and geography. The work of the International Consultancy on Religious Education and Culture (ICOREC) is helpful. This organisation has studied different faiths and (with the Pictorial Charts Education Trust) has produced a series of wall charts on the Rites of Passage of different religions; the final set dealing with Death Rites. It can also be rewarding to talk to those undertakers, celebrants and practitioners who specialise in the intricacies of particular faiths. Whatever religion we have looked at we have found that they all have their passionate advocates and disillusioned doubters so, in an age of individual consumerism, it pays dividends to shop around and make your own judgements.

In many religions there are common concerns and patterns. Just as over 1000 million Christians in the world associate God with light so 500 million Hindus celebrate Divali in October/November with a four or five day Festival of Light.

Hinduism

Hinduism is a Western term for a religious tradition developed over several thousand years in India. In contrast to Christianity, Judaism and Islam it does not trace its origins to one particular founder, has no prophets, no set creed and no particular institutional structure. Although it embraces diverse beliefs and practices with many deities, scriptures and festivals the emphasis is on the right way of living (dharma) rather than a set of doctrines.

The secular and the sacred are not separated as drastically as they are in the West. The spiritual is part of the everyday.

With this holistic approach to life, where the universal force of creation can be seen in the humble and domestic and where the soul never dies but is reincarnated or transmigrated into different shells there is no way in which Hindu death rites could be the same as for a Christian.

A Hindu believes each person is caught in a cycle of many births, deaths and rebirths, so death is not seen as the end of life but as a time of renewal. All adult Hindus are cremated but babies and young children may be buried. Hindus believe that at cremation when the outward form is reduced to ashes, the soul is released to find a new home in a new body. The family avoids contact with the corpse. The mourners have no contact with outsiders, must sleep on the floor and must neither cut their hair nor worship at the temple. The body is washed, wrapped in a cloth and placed inside a coffin. Hindu women have a strong preference for a female doctor during their lifetime. After death, distress is caused if the body is attended by non-Hindus. In India the coffin is tied to a funeral bier and carried on the shoulders of six male relatives, followed silently by other relatives and friends to an open air crematorium. In India this would be done within 24 hours. The presence of the eldest son or the nearest male relative standing by, provides essential witness at the moment of burning.

In India ghee (clarified butter) is poured on to the pyre to help the fire which is lit by by the eldest son. Prayers and hymns are recited which express the belief in reincarnation. In extreme cases there are traditions of the wife throwing herself on her husband's funeral pyre.

On the third day after the cremation the ashes are collected and, if possible, scattered into a river, preferably the holy river Ganga (Ganges).

The next day relatives and friends visit the home of the deceased bringing gifts to comfort the family and saying prayers with them for the peace of the departed soul.

The final ceremony is performed on the eleventh or thirteenth day after cremation. All who attended the cremation and those who were not able to attend offer rice balls and milk to the dead person which are intended to show the spirit that the family are grateful for kind acts performed in his/her life and to help the spirit to its next rebirth. Now the mourners are no longer considered to be unclean and they may return to their normal lives.

Judaism

Judaism teaches that death is not final. According to ancient Jewish tradition the dying or their relatives should recite the words:

> "Hear, O Israel, the Lord our God, The Lord is One"

A confession or prayer for forgiveness is also said. The body is washed according to a strict ritual and then wrapped in a shroud (and, if a man, a prayer shawl) and placed in a simple coffin. No flowers are allowed and the simplicity ensures that in death there is no difference between rich and poor.

Orthodox Jews are always buried ideally within twenty-four hours of death, but those of a more liberal persuasion may choose cremation. When the coffin has been lowered into the grave members of the family and friends shovel earth onto it. A daughter who wished to be at her mother's funeral tells us that women are not allowed to be at the graveside.

In some orthodox households there can be a rending of garments as a gesture of grief, the next of kin remain at home for seven days after the funeral, sitting on low stools barefoot, abstaining from bathing and shaving. Prayers are recited every evening in the presence of a quorum of ten men. There follows a less intense period of thirty days' mourning and in the case of the death of a parent, eleven months.

Islam

Muslims are always buried and never cremated. After death the body should not be touched by non-Muslims. If there is no choice, staff must wear disposable gloves. Muslims believe in a Judgement Day and everlasting Heaven and Hell. Bodies, which are considered to belong to God, are buried as quickly as possible, preferably the day after death. After ritual washing the corpse is wrapped in three pieces of white cotton cloth. In Britain local by-laws often insist that a coffin is used (although this is changing), but in many Muslim countries coffins are not used. The body is buried with the head facing towards Mecca and the grave itself is raised a little above ground to prevent people from walking on it. High gravestones and monuments are forbidden.

Sikhism

Sikhs are always cremated. They wear five symbols of their faith and gifts of money and oil may be thrown into the coffin. In the Punjab the body will be burnt on a funeral pyre but in Britain it is taken to a crematorium and arrangements made so that close male relatives can be present when the body is placed in the furnace. The cremation should take place as early as possible and in India would take place within 24 hours of death. In Britain this is not always possible in busy crematoria so the funeral may need to be delayed for several days.

To a Sikh, birth and death are closely associated as part of the cycle of human life which is seen as a transient stage towards Nirvana, or complete union with God. Heaven and Hell are temporary stages where the soul is rewarded or corrected before it continues the cycle of rebirth. Mourning is therefore discouraged, especially for those who have lived a long and fruitful life and so a funeral may be more obviously a celebration accompanied by brass bands. In India the ashes are sprinkled into a river. As this is not always appropriate in Britain they are often flown back to India and placed into the Ganges.

Buddhism

is a major religion but has no god. It originated in Nepal in the sixth century BC and is now powerful in the Indo-Chinese peninsula (China, Japan and Korea) and is rapidly growing in the West. Buddha, "the Enlightened", is revered more as an example of a way of life than as a god. Although there are many different sects (some of which are very patriarchal) all Buddhists believe in reincarnation and accept responsibility for their behaviour in this life, since the consequences of their actions continue in subsequent lives. As there is no god there is no worship but the act of respect ("Puja") is their way of acknowledging an ideal and searching for inner stillness. In Britain there are at least three different traditions. All show concern for the state of mind at the time of death, believing that this will influence the character of rebirth. Meditation and chanting are possible in death rites but formal ritual requirements in relation to the corpse are minimal. Time from death to disposal is usually from three to seven days.

The Dead Good Funerals Book

Most Buddhists prefer cremation but if the body or ashes are buried a headstone can bear the symbol of the eight spoked wheel of the law.

Miscellaneous Funeral Customs

The variety of funeral customs and superstitions around the world is unbelievable. Nigel Barley's inspirational book **Dancing on the Grave** recounts many and other examples can be found in the St Mungo Museum of Religion in Glasgow:

■ One hundred years ago in Britain infant mortality was so high that the church had to provide hymns and paintings depicting brothers and sisters dancing with Jesus. At that time plaster death masks were made of children whereas now we use photographs to facilitate grieving and maintain memories. These are usually snapshots of the living rather than photographs of the dead.

■ Prehistoric people buried ashes in urns in tumuli.

■ In Minoan Crete bodies were buried in stone or terracotta coffins previously used as baths. Bones were broken after rigor mortis to fit the bodies into a foetal postion.

■ The very well publicised Ghanaian painted carved coffins ... now in demand as exotic novelties for every modern art gallery in the world (as functionless artefacts) ... show that you can be buried in the shape of a chicken, a lion, a cow, a Mercedes, a space shuttle, a Red Arrow or really anything you want, or can afford or choose to embarrass your neighbours with. In Ghana they use big cement-lined graves and the Church rejects the most animistic imagery because it is pagan.

■ Memorials or headstones can vary enormously. In Rumania one local carpenter traditionally carved and painted biographical caricatures on simple wooden crosses for everyone who died in his village.

■ Favourite objects and possessions are often placed in the coffin and buried with the person – workbox, photograph, pipe, tobacco, bottle of whisky, Polo mints. In her poem "Last Words", Sylvia Plath asks to have her copper cooking pots

LAST WORDS
Sylvia Plath

I do not want a plain box, I want a sarcophagus
With tigery stripes, and a face on it
Round as the moon, to stare up.
I want to be looking at them when they come
Picking among the dumb minerals, the roots.
I see them already – the pale, star-distance faces.
Now they are nothing, they are not even babies.
I imagine them without fathers or mothers, like the first gods.
They will wonder if I was important.
I should sugar and preserve my days like fruit!
My mirror is clouding over –
A few more breaths, and it will reflect nothing at all.
The flowers and the faces whiten to a sheet.
I do not trust the spirit. It escapes like steam
In dreams, through mouth-hole or eye-hole. I can't stop it.
One day it won't come back. Things aren't like that.
They stay, their little particular lustres
Warmed by much handling. They almost purr.
When the soles of my feet grow cold.
The blue eye of my turquoise will comfort me.
Let me have my copper cooking pots, let my rouge pots
Bloom about me like night flowers, with a good smell.
They will roll me up in bandages, they will store my heart
Under my feet in a neat parcel.
I shall hardly know myself. It will be dark,
And the shine of these small things sweeter than the face of
Ishtar.

The Dead Good Funerals Book

and rouge pots tucked in around her. Today you might place a mobile telephone in a coffin – but for goodness' sake switch it off!

This multitude of possibilities is overwhelming. We can be so stuck on rigid notions of what a funeral has become that it is refreshing to consider other ways. Would you like to be buried face down, face up, sitting, lying on your side or in a foetal position? Sometimes laws, particularly local by-laws, inhibit innovation and it is not always easy (practically or legally) to do exactly what we would wish. Sometimes it is appropriate to work with existing traditions. But not always. Conservative attitudes and laws will only be changed by people who decide, with good reason, that they need something different. Whatever forms we discover we have to ask what religious beliefs, if any, we need to inform our proposed ceremonies.

Ways of creating new Funeral Ceremonies

We have described funeral experiences that made us question, explored encounters with death, rites of passage and the nature and role of religion in funerals. Next we look at a little more theory and a few hypothetical examples. *But first we must reclaim the sacred.*

A Sense of the Sacred

Mircea Eliade, the historian of world religions, found many common patterns between beliefs. In his classic **The Sacred and the Profane** (1956) many of the words used to describe spiritual experience clearly articulate powerful sights, feelings and occurrences, which can exist outside "religion".

"Awesome, magnificent, moving, mysterious, terrifying, extraordinary, enchanting, strange, cosmic, haunting, weird, magical, amazing, holy", are the kind of adjectives we use to describe special events such as chance meetings, storms, love, works of art, places, dreams, and unusual atmospheres. These adjectives and nouns such as "life, being, existence, harmony, nature, fecundity, discovery, revelation, insight, belief, intuition, truth, energy, transformation, inspiration, vision, infinity", and more are the kind of words associated with "a sense of the sacred". Despite our secular life-style many people experience an instinctive sense of inexplicable wonder. When we allow ourselves to be "in the right frame of mind", when "time seems to stand still", or "the hairs on the back of our neck stand up", when we contemplate, meditate, see ghosts, have premonitions, witness multiple coincidences; "have a sixth sense", "lose ourselves" etc, then we have "a sense of the sacred." We need to gain the confidence to look at our inner feelings and recognise them.

Physical, often solo, activities such as gardening, fishing, sailing, walking and climbing, ski-ing, surfing, many other sports, dancing, singing, primary artistic creation, some work (and play) and some scientific investigations can trigger heightened sensations. This may be no more than adrenaline-driven escapism of course. We all respond differently, but there is a need to leave the mundane and it is not uncommon for people to claim that such activities are "mind expanding", putting them "in touch with something else" when they experience "energy moving through them as if they were only a medium or vehicle".

Trance state dancing in many cultures (including all night raves) is another way we seek spiritual excess. Chemical stimulants can be dangerous of course but then so can religion. Artists, musicians and poets particularly often claim that their creations surprise them and appear from the subconscious or "somewhere outside themselves". Whether they are equally using an artistic alibi to escape or genuinely exploring the edges of perception does vary. However if escapism is required by so many then maybe we need to look at underlying causes.

Chagall is an interesting example of an artist who escaped to his own world but brought back dreams that many enjoy. In the introduction to his series of paintings based on Biblical imagery in the Musée National in Nice he says:

> "In the course of my life I have often had the feeling that I was someone other than myself, that I was born somewhere between heaven and earth, so to speak; the world has always struck me as being one vast desert where my soul wanders like a lighted torch ... As life is an inexorable course towards death

we must enliven it with our own colours of love and
hope. Such love gives life its social cohesion and
religion its essence."

Chagall used the Bible as a source of poetic inspiration and
good stories rather than a literal base of liturgical dogma.
He saw it as a synonym for Nature. Maybe, if we need an
iconography, this is the way to re-incorporate our traditional
religious imagery, as the early Christian Church colonised
existing folk and pagan forms and sites. Even as late as the
end of the 19th century there was a living tradition in some
parts of England that a funeral procession must necessarily go
"the way of the sun", which was probably a remnant of Baal
worship!

Although all "faith" is finally subjective many people use
the word "miraculous" to describe birth, rearing children,
recovering from illness and falling in love. We experience
chance occurrences and strings of good and bad luck which
have an inexplicable but certain logic. Whenever the
particular combination of place, time and image takes on a life
of its own and we are in a state of "heightened awareness",
then we could say we are experiencing the sacred. Our
intuitions speak well and it can be a mistake to try to translate
them into precise codes or rationalisations.

Most often we don't need the presence of a personalised or
personable deity. Such an icon can provide a comfortable
symbol but it can be a substitute. We can discover the
sacred in the everyday outside institutionalised religions.
"Ordinary" people have the capacity for deep intuition and
understand what is truthful. Clear perception and spiritual
well-being stem from inside us. If we can create the right
centre for ourselves and focus clearly and openly then we
can train our consciousness to work on many levels. We may
spot unusual conjunctions and connections, be more aware
of the "inexplicable", positively enjoy what is around us and
generally be more in touch with ourselves.

As I was reading Mircea Eliade about "sacred time and
myths" in a sunlit pavement cafe in Nice a tiny pigeon feather
landed on my notebook. The small grey feather spiralling in
the breeze reminded me of many other things. With the sun
behind it it took on the shape of the Bay of Angels and the
structure of a fish skeleton.

It was of course only a chance feather but it was a timely reminder of infinite pattern. Usually we are too busy to contemplate infinity. Here my "sense of the sacred" was imaginatively triggered and an everyday, quite corny incident had greater meaning. At the time I scribbled in my notebook:

> "The softest grey feather.
> A bay.
> A sky.
> A kiss.
> Canopy of sunlight
> over ribcage of breezes."

This could be the smallest tip of a personal belief system. Centuries ago a better scribe wrote an Egyptian hymn to be sung at a Pharaoh's death ...

> "Thy Mother the Sky reaches forth her arms to thee.
> Now thou art one with thy Mother the Sky."

And what's good enough for a Pharaoh, (and a pigeon), is good enough for me. Except that I don't want to be embalmed because, first I don't want my flesh to be drained of blood (which is flushed down the drain) nor for my appearance to be artificially sustained with formaldehyde (which is a chemical pollutant). Nor to be mummified. Because I think to try to preserve the flesh is an expensive vanity and I don't want to end up in a heritage museum. Nor fired into space; there's enough human detritus up there already.

A recap on ritual:

> "Rituals are the life blood of culture. Celebrations are not practice for some more real kind of action, say pragmatic or economic action, nor are they sublimations for some remembered or more desirable action. In a celebratory moment the ritual action is a deed in which the symbols do not merely point, mean, or recall but embody fully and concretely all that is necessary for the moment ... a public celebration is a rope bridge of knotted symbols strung across an abyss. We make our crossings, hoping the chasm will echo our festive sounds for a moment, as the bridge begins to sway from the rhythms of our dance."   Ron Grimes, Professor of Religion,
> University of Hamilton, Ontario

In a ritual we enact a routine publicly or privately within a tribal group or family, to celebrate or commemorate the occasion within an agreed set of values. We can acknowledge trans-human powers and even invisible phenomena if we believe in them.

In ritual, doing is believing. As the humanists indicate in their efficient booklet on funeral ceremonies: a funeral is not a philosophical discourse, it is an action.

The Funeral of Bryan Fox

This started off as a proposal for my own funeral but as I wrote it I realised I was being far too prescriptive. The dead can't control the living; preliminary suggestions may be useful but a too rigid and obsessive script can generate resentment or even guilt if precise instructions cannot be fully realised. This is especially so in a creative family where everyone might take a role. The best solution is to have early meetings well before the fatal day (or night) and if certain artefacts are deemed crucial then you can make them yourself and store them in a cupboard marked "In case of death"! It can be very therapeutic. You could even sleep in your coffin, or have it (in flatpack form) under your bed ... or maybe use it as a filing cabinet or a bookcase in your office.

For the purpose of demonstrating the process therefore I have invented a twin brother and imagine myself helping to organise his funeral.

White Anglo-Saxon man. Artist and beer drinker. Aged 65. Married. Two children, two grandchildren. Wife surviving. Died peacefully after a stroke. Religion: believed passionately in people. Otherwise romantic nature worshipper with growing interest in science and micro-biology in particular (see postscript).

A belief system is a subjective comprehension of the sacred, presented in a form accessible to others. It underpins the rite. Here is Bryan's:

Prayer at Death

One time there was no time.
Before history got hold of us and we could date the
nails in the cross,
we loved the cycle from seed to blossom to fruit
and ate apples with no worries.
When winter came we hoped and knew
that as the moon waxed and waned balefully
under the eye of the sun,
the beacon would flame again.
We knew our bones held the pattern of mudfish.
That calcium was part of the earth and the stars
and always had been
and always will be.
So when our teeth chatter in cold fear,
the rhythm echoes in Banyan trees.
In acorns
cups and bowls
in urns and earth
the song we strike is the song of Eternity,
which in the spring of creation rises still;
spouting a flood of love
which remains.
As crystals in the eyes of the world
and memories in the gravest night.

This rural ecological fable, the basis of Bryan's belief
structure informs the ritual.

In his will he wrote :

> "After I am certified dead (by two doctors) and
> provided my family are happy about it and if I'm not
> too old (which I probably will be!) my organs can be
> taken to preserve life directly in others. But not for
> medical research. After organ removal I'd like loved
> ones to wash me down (but professionals are ok
> too), sprinkle me with a little clove oil only and wrap
> my corpse in a beautiful thick bright red blanket."

So wrapped in his favourite blanket we placed his body in a
deep blue shiny cardboard coffin painted inside and out. On
the lid his daughter painted simple seed and tree designs in

The Dead Good Funerals Book

white lines. These images were based on his "prayer at death". The coffin rested on trestles in the front room of his house for a day or two; we preferred not to have an open coffin.

"No incense"

he had requested. So we lit a few candles smelling of honey.

The night before the committal his coffin was driven round Ulverston on a flat bed truck. We visited his works and a couple of pubs accompanied by a wild percussion band, with salsa brass and firecrackers; then returned to the house.

We knew he preferred cremation so we negotiated with the crematorium manager for a double slot at the beginning of the day to gain time to decorate the space and take it all down afterwards. We hung the crem' with simple big banners in blue and red suspended from theatrical lighting stands and put marigolds and sunflowers in earthenware vases. We framed it all with strings of small white paper cuts cut with fire and bird imagery and made it more cosy with pools of warm lighting. Incidentally, we did have to remove temporarily a crucifix and cover up a statue depicting a sentimental Jesus story about the sheep that escaped.

Rather unconventionally, we arranged the seats in a circle and placed the coffin on trestles in the middle. On the floor was a bright red Persian carpet (which we borrowed from a shop in town). It looked fantastic. The white seed decorations, painted on the top of the coffin resembled galaxies and the surrounding banners gave the feeling of a womb-like tent. The service was a bit longer than usual because many people wanted to read poems and tell stories. We gave out photocopied sheets of some of his poems and later made a few handmade books as presents for those who had helped.

The music was great. His son, a musical director, arranged a few tunes for cellos, trombone and trumpet with a small a cappella choir who helped us sing along. "What is the Life of a Man" was hung up on a song sheet! Bryan always said he wanted a song sheet at his funeral because no one ever knows the words of the hymns, but really because he was theatrical and loved pantomimes. Painting the words and hanging the banner took so long we nearly had to abandon the idea but it was worth it. As was rehearsing the choir.

There were quite a few readings mainly from texts about art and creativity. For example one was a warning from Eric Fromm (who studied fascism in concentration camps):

> "Failure to make use of our capacity for love and reason results in the development of the reverse; ... we wish to control life absolutely or destroy it."

and the other a quote from **Anatomy of an Illness** by Norman Cousins, the man who allegedly cured himself of cancer by laughing at Marx Brothers films:

> "Death is not the ultimate tragedy of life. The ultimate tragedy is de-personalisation – dying in an alien and sterile area, separated from being able to reach out a loving hand, separated from a desire to experience the things that made life worth living, separated from hope."

The ceremony would have benefited from a master of ceremonies. Bryan had stipulated:

> "There can only be a priest if he or she is prepared to take off their dog collar and officiate as a friend outside the role of Christian and tell the congregation they are doing this."

Even the best vicar we knew said he should not be asked to do this as it compromised his integrity. We have heard of those who don't mind.

We tried to do it between us but there were many awkward moments and it would have been better to have recruited a confident person or series of people used to public speaking who knew a few jokes.

The one thing we did respect was Bryan's request that:

> "Please will someone from my family be present at the incinerator when the coffin and body are consumed."

This was hard. We had, beforehand, looked at the fire boxes or "cremators", as they call them, and thought, frankly, that they looked like Belsen ovens. It nearly put us off the idea of cremation altogether, it was so clinical and industrial. But the staff were so supportive that it was eventually alright. They explained how precise they were with each body and the control of the flues and emission of smoke and gases. There was even a question about the toxicity of the paint we had used on the cardboard coffin but the problem turned out to be minimal.

There was an awkward moment when we had to carry the coffin from the middle of the room to the crematorium rollers before it went through to the back, but we coped. As we had brought the coffin down in the first place in our own estate car we used just the same bearers again. I would have preferred carrying it all the way to the burners because I hate the theatrical altar/stage and curtains of the crem. The incineration took the average one and a half hours to complete.

At the start we fired a few mortar shells outside ... beautiful big red chrysanthemum shells. Stupidly we forgot to tell the police we were doing it, so they screamed up with blue lights flashing. They were OK about it in the end but it cost us a donation to the Police Benevolent Fund (and a bottle of Scotch at Christmas). I reckon Bryan was chuckling "I told you so" in the stars.

Afterwards we all went to our garden for a big tea, and loads of malt whisky. We filled a souvenir scrapbook with comments and drawings, put up a display of old photos and hired a Cajun band.

We collected the ashes the next day (they came in the usual bronzed plastic container) and immediately transferred them to a lidded earthenware urn (a small bread crock), and carefully placed it into a neat circular hole about two feet deep that we'd dug in Bryan's lawn. We were a bit sick of ceremonies by now so we did it in a very matter of fact way, splashed a drop of whisky on top, drank a toast and made a bad joke.

A few weeks later we gathered a few acorns on a walk and planted them nearby. At key anniversaries we light a lantern there too and when any saplings sprout up we'll take one to plant in a secret site. There was also a theory that at the end of our grieving in, say, two or three years' time, we would dig up the urn and (because he liked the metaphor of tides and journeys into the West), take it to the top of Bigland to scatter his ashes over Morecambe Bay at sunset.

Finally we'd use the pot in our garden for displays of wild flowers and herbs including rosemary and thyme. Those were the herbs he used most in cooking and he always said "instructions for a funeral ceremony should be a simple recipe for action".

We have made one mistake though. The ashes in the urn in the garden will get soaked in water and scattering them will be like trying to chuck a lump of pumice stone or grey flapjack in the air. That is if the pot hasn't shattered first with the frost. Either we should have kept them inside or accept we'd have to break the pot and break the crust of ashes. That could work, but the urn could not survive to become a feature in the herb garden.

Ten key reminders

1   We don't legally own our bodies after death. A plan is best devised, therefore, in consultation with relatives and kept flexible. The responsibility for carrying out our wishes lies with our appointed executor. Even if we provide very detailed instructions they can legally do as they wish. In Clint Eastwood's film **Bridges of Madison County** (1995), a brother and sister are horrified to discover from their mother's will that after falling in love with a stranger she requests them to scatter her cremated remains off the bridge where she had met her lover, rather than have her body buried next to their father. At first they refuse, but come to terms with the idea and in the final scenes we see her ashes blowing appropriately.

2   The wishes of the bereaved, who may or may not be the executors, are crucial. A husband may expect that he be buried for ever in the back garden or his ashes riddled in the compost, but this could be a pain for his wife who may not wish to be crowded for ever by his gritty presence. The process of the funeral, the nuts and bolts of the action, even the devising, can be therapeutic and special for the bereaved and decisions should not be taken away from them.

3   The future is always uncertain. It may be possible to plan a funeral during a lengthy terminal illness but we cannot

prescribe for the sudden accident, unexpected illness or death abroad. A decision about cremation or burial may depend upon the state of the body at death. In our society and others the death of a young person is usually regarded as being "unfair or unjust" and in this case relations and friends may need special help. (According to Nigel Barley, the Yoruba people of Nigeria do not allow parents to attend the funerals of their dead children, since it is the children who should bury the parents and it is expected that bereaved parents will be beyond all decent behaviour.) Also, as views about the kind of ceremony we want change with our age and the number and ages of our dependents, it is sensible to give regular updates to our wills.

4   Imaginative ideas should be practical, on the right scale and within your organisational and financial means. Many people imagine a "Viking Funeral", by which they intend a burning long boat voyaging into the sunset. Forget it. In Britain the law would prevent you from burning a body on an open fire, long boats are big and expensive and you'd be a danger to shipping. And burials at sea round the British Isles are unpredictable. See **Sea Burial**.

5   With our western culture and education there is a danger of too much thinking and critical rationalisation. We are steered away from intuition, thinking with our fingers, taking risks and making our own decisions. Individual action and personal confidence are undermined and we look everywhere for experts other than at ourselves.

6   Even if there are customary practices and structures each ritual is a one-off event for the participants.

7   Very little invention is possible in the short time between death and the funeral ceremony and only then if the main principles and structure have already been considered. If we don't think ahead we will end up with ready made inappropriate and expensive packages. Give broad instructions in your will and discuss it beforehand with your executors and celebrant if you plan to have one.

8   There will still be extreme busy-ness round the occasion. This is a natural and necessary way of dealing with deep shock and should be encouraged. However precisely a ritual has been planned there will be more than enough to do.

9   Poetry can be useful because it distances and distills emotion. Many people have their own favourites which should be relevant and accessible at first hearing. The W H Auden poem used at the funeral in the film **Four Weddings and a Funeral** is a good example. It's strong and truthful, but it is a despairing lament and not to everyone's taste. When selecting sermons or poems or hymns decide the basic question:

Is this ceremony a celebration of the life of the deceased or anguished elegy in the face of death? A springboard for the living or memorial of the deceased? Or both?

Epitaph

It is Saturday lunchtime 11th November 1995 and I am researching the final chapter of this book. Reading **Dancing on the Grave**, I copy the following notes:

> *"The symptoms of death – lack of respiration or heartbeat, coldness and rigor mortis, opening of the sphincters, insensitivity to electrical stimuli – may occur without death. The only sure and certain sign of death is the putrefaction of the corpse. In a culture that believes in neither after-life nor reincarnation, memory is the only place left for identity to go."*

Suddenly there is a newsflash on the radio in my office:

> *"In the Himalayas twenty-six trekkers have been killed in an avalanche. Camp completely submerged under many feet of snow. In the Gyoko valley near the Everest slopes."*

As luck would have it – Sue and Hannah (my wife and daughter) are at this moment on a trekking holiday in the Himalayas, destination Manang, in Nepal. Pathological optimist that I am, irrational superstitions take over. A nightmare twenty-four hours begins. My diary continues:

Panic. Check guide books and eventually calculate that Everest is 160 miles from Manang. Double check with Ceefax. 3.30 pm:

> "NEPAL: Fifteen confirmed dead in avalanche. This follows earlier reports quoting a rescue worker who said twenty-six were confirmed dead. Among the dead were thirteen Japanese trekkers and Sherpas camping SW of Mount Everest when the avalanche struck last night."

It's not you. And a twinge of sadness (and guilt) for the bereaved. But then immediately a new item flashes up:

> "Meanwhile eight walkers have died in a landslide in the Manang area of the NW Himalayan Range."

6pm News confirms this:

> "Of the eight who died, four were Nepalese and four were non-Nepalese. One a Canadian. The other three bodies have not been identified, and nationality not yet determined, but one was a woman."

According to rational calculation this could easily be you two setting off. Horrible images and paranoid connecting of every sign and memory. Light the Japanese lantern in your office, hold the tiny stone which rests on the keyboard of our wooden angel playing a harmonium, press my hands onto the two cloth prints of the flying woodcocks (copies of the ones that I had given you as gifts for your journey) and peruse photos on my wall. Spend an hour checking/guessing your route. Is this praying? Examine the photos of you on my desk; the ones you took in your trekking gear and hope that I won't have to use them to identify your bodies. That's if you're not buried under mud.

Huge panic. Listen to all news broadcasts and check Ceefax at every opportunity. 4.45pm buy Rescue Remedy and check the office to see if there is a fax. Listen all through the night to BBC World Service News: "Avalanches and *mud* slides." Get two hours' sleep thanks to whisky and Rescue Remedy.

Wonder what prayer is. Think cardboard coffins, ceremonies, future of our work together, Daniel, love and journeys etc. Especially the song Pete suggested for the Funeral book and sang to me on *Friday*, (mudslide day), which is about a journey coming to an end.

There is also a massive public mood of death and requiem in the air because this year is the fiftieth anniversary of the end of the Second World War and veterans are asking us to stand in silence today to commemorate the 11th hour of the 11th day of the 11th month, when the First World War came to an end.

Sunday morning 8am: New message on Ceefax:

"The death toll now stands at 43."

Telephone BBC for more details from previous day's **World at One** report which had been so specific. "We haven't heard of any British deaths, but ring the Foreign Office." Tried three times. No reply.

10.50am. Go to the office to see if there is a fax. *No*. Do loads of photocopying as a distraction. Then just as an afterthought try the answer machine. Incredibly there is your message.

4.45pm Sunday afternoon, 10.45am our time, sounding so cheery, saying you have come down from the mountain snow and will be in Pokhara in nine to ten days. Play it four times over. Amazing. Shout for Joy.

All the terrible deaths were on Friday and Saturday. Unless ghosts giggle and don't know what to say in remote Nepalese post offices you're *safe* and judging by your mood probably know nothing about the mudslides. (I learned when you returned that if Hannah had not been ill for a day, which delayed your start you would have, indeed, been in that fated village.) As luck would have it.

How the nightmare would have run if I hadn't heard your voices. But you are both alive. Magic. All so unreal this experiencing through information machines, transcripts and bulletins on the hour with news that disappears.

My current "horrorscopes" (pathetic how I started to read them) keep emphasising "transformation" and a major threshold point. I have learned something about needing to live in the moment. It's hard to stop the mind racing on the worst scenario. Too overworked and neurotic an imagination

was a disturbing but intriguing reminder of just how much such visual relics have become commonplace. ("Memory the only place left for identity to go.") Maybe they make it easier for us to frame loss than it was for previous generations?

Barley makes the point that "even in our photo-loving society, the last scene of the family album, the funeral, is always missing". Camcorders are common place at christenings and weddings so why not at funerals? As they were for Alison Hargreaves' public memorial service on television. Or is a funeral the one time when we want to be with our own inner emotions and not distance them with a camera or a simplified image?

The children heard stories and drew trees with leaves falling. Regeneration and change is all. Nothing stands still. Sorrow and grief are our own. We can share them. We heal and accommodate loss but it never goes away for good. We get angry and scribble angry trees. Above all we should not let it fester unnoticed inside.

Finally as the family sat alone before the distant K2, where she died, we (and the camera crew) were privileged to eavesdrop. The children had made delicate drawings of the fierce mountain. The little girl clutched silk flowers she had brought all the way from grandma. Jim Ballard spotted a wraith of a cloud hovering above the peak. "Is that mummy?" said Kate. "Her spirit is off climbing in these mountains," said her Dad. And they placed their offerings in a small cairn. "Can I put a sweetie there too, for mummy?" asked Kate.

After a long hard journey and an immense loss this ... tiny simple resolution. It was a rare gift for us to be sharing airwaves just then. A rare lesson too. If Death is always there, but it's too hard to contemplate all the time, when it does come to our relatives and friends (never mind ourselves) a focussed physical pilgrimage, practical forms of externalisation and clear simple images and objects can help us channel our emotion. This may seem obvious but unfortunately the right ceremony doesn't always materialise and it can be useful to think about it beforehand.

It was Tom the six year old who convinced his father to undertake the pilgrimage we were told. Probably he knew instinctively what he needed and as far you can judge from the fabric of dispassionate film it seemed to work.

For me it earthed my Nepal experience, taught me how much we can trust our earliest instincts, how much we need ritual structures and how helpful it is for us all to discover and share simple honest poetry.

To be alive is to die. To understand death we need support. If we can participate in grief through electronic networks of virtual communities and genealogical trees we may find new channels for new rites where shared grief can transform to shared laughter. Death will always remain but if we face it, then maybe we'll dance longer together on the edge and our epitaph will be:

> I never got out of this world alive
> But while I was there
> I sure jumped and jived.

Postscript – October 2003

A report in the magazine *Nature* quoted in *The Independent* 24th October 2003 suggests that manipulation of the genes and hormones of a nematode worm increases their life six-fold. "These findings show that remarkable life span extensions can be produced with no apparent loss of health or vitality (except the reproductive organs had to be removed to conduct the experiment!). Applied to humans the equivalent would indicate we could live for 500 years."

Given our knowledge-based consumer culture driven by money, this implies that rich people may soon enough be able seriously to extend their lives and pretend that death has been eradicated. A funeral every 500 years would seriously affect the form of such a ceremony (never mind sales of this book!)

"One Rock", Welfare State International's 2003 site-specific art installation at Lanternhouse, is an ecological triptych based on the macro, micro and mythic aspects of one particular rock in Morecambe Bay. In our research we discovered the inspirational **What is Life?** by Lynn Margulis and Dorian Sagan (University of California Press – paperback – published 2000). "One Rock" is set in the liminal space between land and sea (the space where "transition and transformation" is the daily norm rather than the substance of occasional rituals or intentional art).

What is Life? has made us aware of pre-human species like microbes, who are part of us and with whom we exist in a mutually dependent symbiotic relationship. We are, it appears, connected with all other living beings (including Planet Earth) in a continuous generational evolution of our immortal genes and chemical imprints. In giving us a "cosmic recipe for life" defined by thermodynamic equilibrium, Margulis and Sagan demonstrate that our bodies have virtually the same chemistry as that prevailing on the Earth's surface 3,000 million years ago, so:

"Death is illusory in quite a real sense. As sheer persistence of biochemistry 'we' have never died during the passage of 3,000 million years. Mountains and seas and even super continents have come and gone, but we have persisted."

AMEN ... INDEED

Funeral Directors' Supplies List:

APRONS - all types • BARRIER P, when dealing with infection • BLE form • BODY BAGS - in two differen rubber • BUCKETS - stainless MATERIALS - a good selection general or preproom use • COSM types • COTTON WOOL - both BP DEODORANTS - in liquid or spray LAMPS - full range of perfumes av POUCHES - several different t DISINFECTANTS - many different ty

MATERIAL - books and charts for embalmers • EMBAL - a full range • EMBALMING POWDER - help control u EYEWASH UNITS - for protection of staff, embalmers or POWDER - useful in presentation • FIRST AID KITS - to legislation • FIRST CALL KITS - 2-man type for mess TRAYS - in fibreglass • FUNERAL DIRECTORS' PRESI you need for presentation • FUNERAL DIRECTORS' 1 storing items used for closing coffins, etc. • GLASSES - pro • GRAVEMARKERS - temporary, in black or white finish - for protection of the living! • GOGGLES HIBISCRUB - for hand disinfection • HEADRESTS - in fibreg prevents mix-ups with remains • IDENTIFICATIO to collect stillborns • INFANT REMOVAL BOX • INSTRUMENTS - a full range available • INSTRUMEN LIQUID - for care of instruments • JEWELLERY BOX - for family • JUMBO ROLLS AND STANDS - for use in prepro KIDNEY DISHES - for use in preproom • LIGATURES - for etc. • LIQUID SOAP AND DISPENSERS - - many different types

IN BLACKWATER WOODS
Mary Oliver

Look, the trees
are turning
their own bodies
into pillars

of light,
are giving off the rich
fragrance of cinnamon
and fulfilment,

the long tapers
of cattails
are bursting and floating over
the blue shoulders

of the ponds,
and every pond,
no matter what its
name is, is

nameless now.
Every year
everything
I have ever learned

in my lifetime
leads back to this: the fires
and the black river of loss
whose other side

is salvation,
whose meaning
none of us will ever know.
To live in this world

you must be able
to do three things:
to love what is mortal;
to hold it

against your bones knowing
your own life depends on it:
and, when the time comes to let
it go,
to let it go

PART FIVE
OTHER SOLUTIONS
Advance funeral wishes

The process of committing to paper ideas about one's own funeral stimulates debate and the thinking process. Some people will include these wishes in their Will, but that is frequently not read until after the funeral has taken place. Make sure people close to you are aware of any document you have created pertaining to your own funeral, and know where it can be found. It is wise to file a copy with your solicitor.

Funeral wishes are not legally binding, although most people endeavour to follow them, if they are seen as reasonable and achievable.

Avoid being too controlling. It is essential that those who are undertaking the funeral arrangements feel they have space to make some contribution of their own. The funeral is, after all, for them.

Begin with factual information:

■ Name and contact details of next of kin, and those people you wish to be notified of your death.

■ Information on any pre-paid funeral plan.

■ Do you choose burial or cremation?

■ Any organ or body donation scheme in place?

■ Any burial plot already purchased or reserved? If not, preferred kind of burial ground, where appropriate.

■ Preference for type of coffin: traditional, willow, cardboard, pine, decorated or not.

■ Location of any urn or coffin or shroud already made or purchased.

GOODBYE
Pauline Prior-Pitt

and did you know
that this
would be
your Deathday
you had not
been told
how ill.
you were not
involved
it was not
happening.
we were to
keep it
from you.

pretending
as always
and were you
keeping it
did you long
to cry out
I'm dying
yet say
nothing
you must have known

and did you
wonder
how we'd be
without you
and did you
feel afraid
and couldn't say
and did you
long to hold
to hold us
to you and say goodbye
goodbye

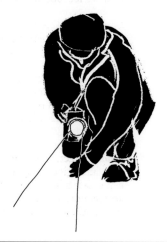

- Views on embalming.

- Name of anyone already approached to organise the funeral.

- Thoughts on funeral arrangements: secular or religious; who might lead it; where to hold it; who might attend; list of publications in which death announcements are to be made.

- Suggestions for the content of the ceremony: writings and music you like; philosophical or spiritual beliefs to be reflected. Give guidance as to where people might look, but leave some of the final choices to them.

- After the funeral: tree planting; scattering of ashes in a favourite place; memorial gathering; information on any funds set aside for these purposes.

Put your feelings in a letter

Complaining seems to come more naturally than praising. Having a row or an argument makes us articulate but in the moment of wishing to pay compliments, many of us are reduced to inadequate mumbling.

We find it hard to say what we really mean. To tell our nearest how much we love them, what part they play in our life and how we feel about that. Leaving it until it's too late is awful.

Writing it rather than saying it is easier for some people. The feelings are there in their head without doubt, but sharing them, is something else altogether.

This can be communicating from man to woman, from woman to man, from woman to woman, from man to man, from child to parent, from parent to child, from sister to brother, etc etc, family, friends, whoever.

Take the opportunity to write the letter before too long. Write it *now* in fact, use it later. You can decide when or how. To post it, to give it, to 'hide' it to be found. Or alternatively, you can create a 'letterbox' in the household, a jewellery box, a special pot ... where such statements can be left from time to time addressed to someone particular. Create your own.

**Painting the Swiss Cardboard Coffin for a Lover of the Sea – July 1993
– Some thoughts from my notebook**

DAY 1

The coffin arrives packed flat, and you assemble it in the same way almost, that you would assemble a mask on the back of a corn flakes packet. I could not resist seeing what it was like to be inside. Being cardboard it was not very claustrophobic. The coffin looked very bleak and tacky at this stage. It's a different shape at the top than I expected. I don't feel at ease with it. It looks like a bad theatre prop ... I felt a lot better about it when I had painted a white ground all over.

I am looking at this work from two perspectives:

1   Delight at being asked to paint it. A very traditional, useful and beautiful opportunity, when as an artist in the society you are aware of art consistently being marginalised – a very matter of fact attitude.

2   It's like being suddenly thrown into a deep pool. Trying to connect with my own subconscious on a serious naked level to find images that are right. I am also aware that I have a very muddled attitude to death, and ceremonies of death. I suppose I don't exactly come from a culture that recognises death (it tries not to think about it).

I want this coffin to just wrap lightly round you. Imagine it only holding you very gently, like you hold a bird. Cradling. This is one lovely thing about this coffin – no nails, no hardness, hardly closed in. I wonder if your soul goes out by your feet – when I was very ill once, I could feel over some hours, the fever going from my head first, until it was only in my legs, and then my toes, and then it had gone.

DAY 2

Defining how to paint the coffin. I have one side and one end and the top sorted – except for the bird image – I think the bird is too informal – strange thing that.

DAY 3

We had this morning a decision to make about whether we should show the coffin painting in progress to a group of elderly people who are visiting this afternoon. They used to be pupils here when Lanternhouse (WSI's headquarters) was a school ... Sue decided, by the time they got to the room where I was working, that it was fine to show them.

They were very interested and thought it an excellent idea to have cardboard coffins, and save trees, and especially to have your own coffin painted for you, how you wanted it with things painted on it that were important to you.

DAY 4

7.00am   Been awake for ages, dreaming. I feel I have got sort of indigestion about the coffin. It's made me ask too many questions. I need to stand outside all the coming and going of different thoughts and perspectives. Take a look from further back. This is the day to make final decisions about content and overall design and statement.

DAY 5

Very matter of fact now. It's just lovely, painting. It is completely my own now (from the blank cardboard thing at the beginning) and I am at ease with it.

rules; maybe the transaction is never discussed, maybe the reply contains an invitation to meet somewhere for a cup of tea and a chat or a bottle of wine ... Only, don't make them anonymous. Feelings for someone written down *and* shared are valuable and lasting. Raymond Carver wrote simple and direct poetry as he approached his death – "No Need", for example.

Discussing the diagnosis of a terminal illness in the family is impossible for some people. Broaching the subject is the hardest part. Maybe a letter distances it a little and helps in getting started. Pauline Prior-Pitt's poem "Goodbye" deals with this unspoken business in her direct style.

A Daughter arranges her Mother's Funeral

Cardboard coffins are made from largely recycled materials and have been developed using the experience of funeral directors, cemetery and crematorium staff and the packaging industry, to offer a well finished product which is strong, safe and suitable for both burial or cremation – they produce little pollution and are a green alternative for people with environmental concerns. They are simple, inexpensive yet dignified, and are very straightforward to decorate. Painting a coffin can make it absolutely personal, and can be a way to begin to celebrate the life that has ended, with imagery that relates to the person.

Recently Elaine, a colleague, got in touch, asking for help to find a cardboard coffin and an artist to paint it. Her mother had recently been diagnosed as having a terminal illness and her health was deteriorating rapidly, so speed was of the essence. She had seen pictures of our painted coffins, and had memories of an horrendous experience when she was widowed young, with very, very high funeral expenses.

Her ideas were already clearly formed. She would like an artist to paint irises on the coffin. On the sides they were to appear to be growing. On the top they were to look as if they were scattered. Iris was her mother's name. This is a person, with talent and interest in art, currently undergoing training, but the shock of her mother's sudden diagnosis needed to get someone else to carry this out.

We were able to contact an artist in the same region who was interested and available to take this on. They met and discussed the commission, which helped a lot. A ready assembled cardboard coffin was delivered from the supplier overnight.

As the artist got down to work in her workshop over the next four days, two things happened. Iris died, and the plans for the funeral began to be made. Elaine had discussed the idea of the painted coffin with her two sisters before going ahead. They thought it was a lovely idea and encouraged her to do it. There was one elderly relative in the family and Elaine made sure she told her what she was doing. Although a bit apprehensive, she found everyone greeted it as a wonderful idea. "Irises are beautiful. How can people be offended?"

She felt expense was not the key issue, more important was the sense of being in charge of something and turning sadness into something joyful. The more personal she and her sisters made the funeral for their mother, the better it was for them. Losing her mother unexpectedly was a huge trauma, yet she found that saying no to the undertaker who wanted to supply a coffin and insisting on doing things her own way made her begin to feel more in control of her life again.

Another sister was busy organising rehearsals between a pianist and a tenor, who was to sing their mother's favourite popular song during the service.

The day before the funeral Elaine and the artist went together with the completed coffin to the undertakers. An eleventh-hour problem had arisen about lining the cardboard coffin. Although it was not necessary in a strictly functional sense, Elaine understandably felt she wanted to cushion the body of her mother, and the standard linings that are usually stapled into coffins were not necessarily suitable. There was a possibility that the artist might dress the inside with fabric, but time was a problem, and that is a separate job from painting. Over the telephone we discussed quilts and duvets, special shawls or blankets that belonged to Elaine's mother, and she was able to arrive at a solution that she felt at ease with.

The "Iris" coffin, painted by Catriona Stamp.

The undertaker brought Elaine's mother in her coffin to rest overnight in the house before the funeral. "Absolutely beautiful; not at all morbid. It felt like a gift to me."

Changing the style and design of a coffin means also thinking about the flowers and what sort of presentation is appropriate. The florist had been asked to prepare something really natural, irises, of course, and mimosa – no stiff carnations. She brought the flowers to the house and Elaine just opened the door of the room where the coffin stood. She found it stunning, and welcomed the idea. Working closely with

The Dead Good Funerals Book

funerals, the florist had begun to feel a change was due, but had not known how to go about it. This was one possibility.

Elaine took photographs of the coffin in the house and promised one to the florist. A couple of days earlier the artist wanted to take pictures of the completed commission before it left her premises. It was a fine morning and she took the empty coffin out into her garden very early. During the process she noticed that the sunshine had brought out the bees and one in particular insisted on landing on the coffin!

A week or two later Elaine sent us some photographs and wrote:

> "... I think you'll agree Mum's coffin looks pretty stunning. I think it's very important to be able to use an artist in whom one has total confidence and who is sensitive to the brief and occasion, as yours was ..."

Duncan Copley

My hands-on interest in this area of work began when I was asked to make a coffin for a child who was to be cremated within the week. Prior to this, carrying a coffin, lowering it into the earth and the scattering of ashes was the closest I had come to any involvement in the creation of a funeral ceremony.

The coffin I made had a rawness, but radiated a delicacy and simplicity. Hand carved from English lime, I chiselled a seed pod, a nut, a foetal nest that would cocoon the baby. The interior remained rippled from the tool, the exterior became a smooth skin that was stroked by the children present at the funeral as we said our farewells. The process of this making felt entirely sacred. The focus I gave to its creation intensified as the day drew near until into the final hour the charging of an energy into the vessel was tangible as I burnished the outer surface to a flawless creamy sheen with the shavings of lime gathered from the workshop floor. I believed that the energy I exerted from the labour of work would help the release of a spirit that was departing. I had made a vessel for the journey of life from this place in time to another, a vessel that could contain a love, joy and the wild energy of a newborn child. During the labour I was filled with the question of where does the spirit go to?

This experience informed my contribution to the DEAD exhibition, COOMBE. A container for ashes. I have made another vessel also carved from Common Lime, sourced from an ancient sacred site, the churchyard at Hutton Roof near Kirkby Lonsdale. In the heart of the vessel is a secret vault – a gilded chamber –

The Dead Good Funerals Book

just large enough to hold the cremated remains of a person. The ashes are poured into the interior through a channel from the outside. Finally the channel is sealed. COOMBE is an object for contemplation. Sited in a garden or a wilderness it too will decay, in time.

SO MANY DIFFERENT LENGTHS OF TIME
Brian Patten

Cuanto vive el hombre por fin? Vive mil dias o uno solo?
Una semana o varios siglos? Por cuanto tiempo muere el hombre?
Que quiere decir 'para siempre'?
Preocupado per este asunto me dedique a aclarar las cosas.
- Pablo Neruda

How long is a man's life, finally?
Is it a thousand days, or only one?
One week, or a few centuries?
How long does a man's death last?
And what do we mean when we say, 'gone forever'?

Adrift in such preoccupations, we seek clarification.
We can go to the philosophers,
but they will grow tired of our questions.
We can go to the priests and the rabbis
but they might be too busy with administrations.

      *   *   *

So, how long does a man live, finally?
And how much does he live while he lives?
We fret, and ask so many questions –
then when it comes to us
the answer is so simple.

A man lives for as long as we carry him inside us,
for as long as we carry the harvest of his dreams,
for as long as we ourselves live,
holding memories in common, a man lives.

His lover will carry his man's scent, his touch;
his children will carry the weight of his love.
One friend will carry his arguments,
another will hum his favourite tunes,
another will still share his terrors.

And the days will pass with baffled faces,
then the weeks, then the months,
then there will be a day when no question is asked,
and the knots of grief will loosed in the stomach,
and the puffed faces will calm.
And on that day he will not have ceased,
but will have ceased to be separated by death.
How long does a man live, finally?

A man lives so many different lengths of time.

The first four or five lines of the poem are a translation from Pablo Neruda. The translation is by a friend of mine Lucia Graves. The rest of the poem attempts to answer those lines. When I first read the poem on BBC Radio the phone lines were flooded with people wanting a copy. It touched a nerve in so many people who had lost a loved one. I was trying to articulate in the poem my own feelings for a friend who had recently died, and in doing so was reminded of something very simple: we are both many and one. Many people have used the poem at services of various kinds, changing gender, adding names and cutting bits out – the poem is a blue-print, use it how you wish. It was first published in a book called Armada, mainly a collection of poems about my mother's death, which Flamingo published a few years ago now.

Contemporary Rites of Passage

A Lorry Driver's Funeral

The coffin passing along the M54 at the head of the cortège yesterday   *Photograph: Roland Leon*

Lorry takes Keith Hart on his last motorway journey

KEITH HART, a lorry driver, lived in Telford new town, Shropshire, and died of leukaemia at the age of 42.

"I'm more at home in a lorry than a hearse," he had told his wife, Brenda. So yesterday they strapped his coffin on the back of an open-topped lorry and the cortège formed up behind it on the road at the bottom of his garden.

"He really loved the road," said Mrs Hart. "He just loved that work. He couldn't have been locked up in a factory or doing shop work. It's odd that he would have loved every minute of this."

Some of the mourners had met him on CB radio, which he had used long ago when it was illegal. There he had called himself "Windjammer", a name full of freedom to dream of while tailing through a traffic jam on the M1.

"He was a happy, jolly man," said his friend Chris Berrington. "He was very brave in the way he bore his illness. They said he should have died last Christmas time. Everyone who came across Keith" — he passed, shirting around a clickel, trying to find words that meant something — "He was a very well-liked man."

The cortège that formed up behind his coffin looked ordinary,

By Andrew Brown
Religious Affairs Correspondent

except for one fat man with a large ear-stud who turned up talking on a car phone at the wheel of a two-tone Rolls-Royce.

They pulled out in good order, following the route that Keith Hart must have taken every day of his working life. Nothing seems to remain of the villages around Telford except the names of the roundabouts that link the new estates, but at last they swung on to the M54.

About 25 cars followed the two lorries at the head of the procession, slowly and cautiously. Drivers kept their distances, signalled in good time and made room for one another. It was a curious fellowship that must have been quite invisible to the frustrated strangers pouring past in the fast lane. It may have been something of the comradeship that he had felt as a lorry driver and that he wanted his friends to go on feeling.

And so we came to the outskirts of Wolverhampton in the greasy Midlands rain. When the coffin stopped at the BP truck stop, dwarfed by big articulated

lorries from Co Landranders Boroughbridge and London there was a breech of photographers and even a television crew that had been lurking.

Inside the café, Keith's favourite, the mourners drank huge mugs of tea and nibble biscuits in the lorry drivers' bar. The coffin remained outside strapped to the lorry, unattended. Then his friends posed with the coffin for the photographer, touching their friend in respect as he had requested. One of them number videoed the scene.

The cortège returned along the motorway to Telford, where Keith was laid to rest in the graveyard of St Michael's parish church.

The gathering in a windy car park had been a much more genuine ritual of the modern town toyside than any 300-year-old football game played with a pig' bladder. While following the coffin it occurred to me that it is for ries and not ploughmen that shape the countryside today and it is constantly being remodelled for their benefit, and ours.

The community that matters is in the mind or the heart; there was far more in a truck stop on park than you could find in the suburbs of a new town.

In 1993 Keith Hunt, a lorry driver, died of leukaemia in his early 40s. He had lived a year longer than predicted and in that time planned his own funeral, with his wife, to celebrate his love of the road. It was reported, with interest and respect, in the national press.

He wanted his coffin transported on the back of a flat bed truck, via the route he drove every working day of his life along the M54. He wanted the funeral procession to pull into his usual truck stop for a last mug of tea together, before driving on to the graveyard.

These ideas are startling and amusing and at the same time so strong, because of their fundamental consistency and integrity. This has to be a true ritual for the 1990s for this man and his family and his work-mates. It takes honesty to say you're more at home in a lorry than a hearse and courage to put the notion into action, particularly on the part of his widow, who made his last journey so particular.

The support of family and colleagues following in twenty-five cars (some he had met over CB radio in the early days) showed how strong the network was and how appropriate the idea was.

Is it the mark of a good funeral to call up the thought that the deceased would have loved it?

Funeral cortège for driving instructor Mr Arthur Hall, Barrow-in-Furness 2003

Farewell to our milkman

A MILK float carried the body of popular milkman Tony Ronson to Aylesbury cemetery on Wednesday afternoon.

The vehicle was driven from the Holy Trinity Church in Walton Street by his close friends Glen Beck and Allan Luff, of Ron Miller Dairies, where Mr Ronson worked for 20 years.

"All Tony lived for was his job. The idea of using the milk float would have appealed to him," said Mr Beck.

Many of the 100-or-so people present at the service, where Ron Miller gave an address, followed the float on the short trip to the Tring Road cemetery.

One of Mr Ronson's favourite songs, My Way, by Frank Sinatra, played as the congregation left the church.

Mr Ronson, who was 35, died after a chip pan fire at his home in Coronation Villas, Aylesbury, on February 9.

● Above: One of the many floral tributes
● Left: Mr Ronson

● The milk float arrives at Holy Trinity Church in Aylesbury

The body of milkman Tony Ronson is carried to the cemetery on the back of his milk float. Aylesbury, 1997

Tracing a thread through death and life

Since beginning this kind of work, we get telephone calls and letters from strangers asking for advice about a problem they are facing to do with a funeral. They are people who have never heard of Welfare State International, but a friend has told them that they must get in touch.

One such call was from Jean in Liverpool concerning a couple who were friends of hers – Mary (a mature woman with a grown-up family) and David, her partner, who was in the advanced stages of a terminal illness. There was to be a wedding and he was expected to die two weeks after. Jean, the friend, needed a lot of support; she was anxious and finding it all very difficult. I had made my list of questions and ideas and here I quote from my notebook of 3rd December 1994.

"Will the wedding be at the bedside? When is it? Will other people be there? Will there be any kind of 'invitation'?" I'm thinking of four things to suggest:

- tiny lantern on a cane at the foot of the bed

- a special covering for the bed-ceremonial

- delicate white paper cuts for the window

- something printed on paper for an invitation/order of service.

I feel it's important, in the circumstances of a death-bed marriage, for there to be something tangible for the surviving partner to have, in the cruelty of circumstances where something is given and then immediately snatched away. We speak, after three failed attempts, on Saturday morning. The wedding will be a week today. Yes, at the bedside. There's no possibility of movement. There will be others there. Jean tells me she has experience of mounting events in a Liverpool park where people put their memories onto leaves and burnt them, but that does not feel appropriate here.

I start to go through my list. Why not make a tiny lantern? Yes, she could do that. There could be imagery on it, printed onto the tissue paper before it was applied to cover the lantern. Yes, she began as a silk screen artist.

Well, how about fabric? Print a piece of fabric to spread over the bed for the ceremony. After all, all we have to work with is the room, the bed, the window. Poppy heads are a favourite image of Jean's – how about the same image on the fabric as on the lantern? Jean had already suggested to her friend that maybe she could help with some sort of a card – that could have the same imagery on it, she realises.

He is a classical scholar. We talk about trying to find some visual imagery that would resonate for him, drawn from the classical tradition. Jean was nervous about how to find out, shortage of research time etc. Why not ask to look at, to handle, a few of his favourite books? In my mind's eye I can see an etching as the frontispiece – leaves, garlands, maybe laurel (or do I mean wreaths?) Leaves, tree, tree of life – is it appropriate? Winter tree, long shadows.

She tells me the family is planning to have a party at home in the evening, so we agree that something present at the wedding ceremony could transfer to the house – the lantern, the paper cuts ... It seems important to link. We talk about bringing death into life, so we can accept it and go on living.

Then Jean adds the unexpected. One of the grown-up daughters is pregnant. The family is fully aware of the cyclical nature of things – life/death/new life. Now we're on a roll ... these objects, whatever they may be, can have a continued existence in this family. Is the lantern re-lit at the naming of the child? Does the fabric from the wedding ceremony have a role? We weren't clear, at that moment, but as I write this the truth is obvious – might it be his shroud? The family will work all that out for themselves.

By now Jean is a different person. Suddenly it all seems attainable. The toll of losing a close friend is taking more from her than she realised. She will set out to make just one thing, and the joy of the process, getting lost in the tactile part of it, the fabric, the paint, the paper, will be a healing process for her anyway. If she makes two things it will be a bonus. She's relieved. It's all come to within manageable proportions. She feels positive and the energy is coming back. I have no idea what she will do, but it doesn't matter. She wants to let me know afterwards. A family facing a wedding, a funeral and a birth all in one short space of time.

Taking death into life and back again.

Jean sent us a card afterwards. She made two lanterns with little brass bells shivering on fine floristry wire at the top and white torn cotton tassels at the bottom, garlanded with rose hips and vinca which was in flower, hung from hooks in the ceiling so they could turn.

> "David's face definitely was grinning. They have the right amount of imagery which can be interpreted as the viewer wishes. Many thanks."

THE MINISTER

Anne Stevenson

We're going to need the minister
to help this heavy body into the ground.

But he won't dig the hole;
others who are stronger and weaker will have to do that.
And he won't wipe his nose and his eyes;
others who are weaker and stronger will have to do that.
And he won't bake cakes or take care of the kids –
women's work. Anyway,
what would they do at a time like this
if they didn't do that?

No, we'll get the minister to come
and take care of the words.

He doesn't have to make them up,
he doesn't have to say them well,
he doesn't have to like them
so long as they agree to obey him.

We have to have the minister
so the words will know where to go.

Imagine them circling and circling
the confusing cemetery.
Imagine them roving the earth
without anywhere to rest.

How to make a
Lantern

1 What you will need:

A   withies (willow sticks)
B   masking tape
C   gaffer tape
D   scissors
E   pliers
F   candles
G   bottle tops
H   thin wire
I   strong tissue paper (must be "wet strength" tissue paper)
J   PVA glue
K   piece of sponge/foam rubber

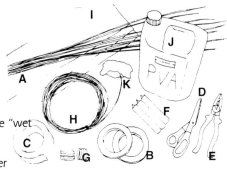

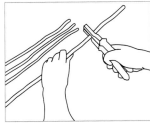

2 Cut four withies the same length for the base.

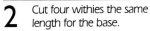

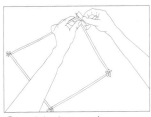

3 Join them at the corners with masking tape.

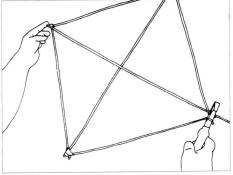

4 Add two diagonals.

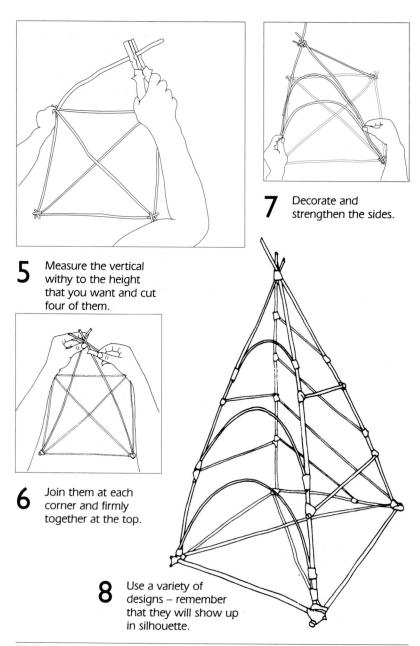

7 Decorate and strengthen the sides.

5 Measure the vertical withy to the height that you want and cut four of them.

6 Join them at each corner and firmly together at the top.

8 Use a variety of designs – remember that they will show up in silhouette.

The Dead Good Funerals Book

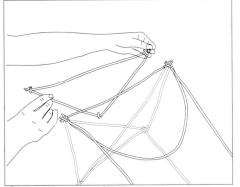

You must not use candle-lit lanterns indoors!

9 Make a door the same shape as one of your sections – either in the base or low down on one side.

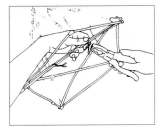

10 Fix it on with wire hinges.

12 Use one piece of wire (approximately 1 metre long). First twist one end of the wire around the candle ...

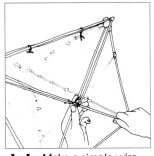

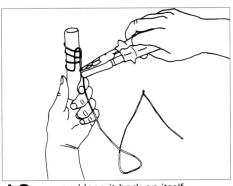

11 Make a simple wire hook to close the door.

13 ... and loop it back on itself.

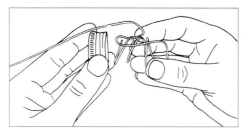

14 Fix it into a bottle top.

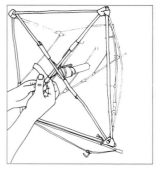

16 ... and attach them very firmly with gaffer tape to the base. There must be 12in (300mm) clear above the flame. **If the lantern is to be used indoors you should substitute a battery torch for the candle.**

Disclaimer: Whilst all due care has been taken in the preparation of this information, neither the authors, nor Welfare State International, nor its members, officers, associates or employees can be held responsible for any omissions contained herein, nor for any damage or injury arising from any interpretation of its contents, howsoever caused.

15 Bend the rest of the wire into four arms ...

17 Many other shapes are possible. Here are a couple.

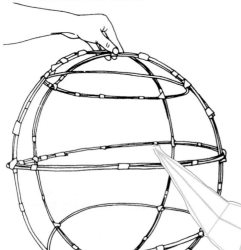

The Dead Good Funerals Book

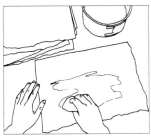

18 Cover your table with plastic. Mix PVA with water (until it runs off the stick). Tear the tissue paper into manageable pieces. On the table spread the PVA over the whole piece of paper with the sponge.

19 Apply the wet tissue to the lantern, overlapping each piece as you go.

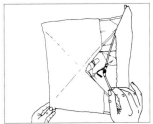

20 Cover the door separately so that it still opens.

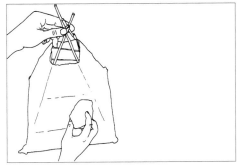

21 Cover the base and the sides, **leaving a gap at the top (above the flame) to let the heat out**. A final coating of PVA will strengthen the whole lantern.

22 Add a wire loop above the candle, and you will need a pole with a hook (gaffer taped on) for carrying your lantern. **If you are using lanterns outdoors with candles and a lantern catches fire then try to ensure that it is away from inflammable materials (eg foliage and trees) and then allow it to burn out. You should not wear a shell suit or nylon anorak.**

How to make a
Paper Cut

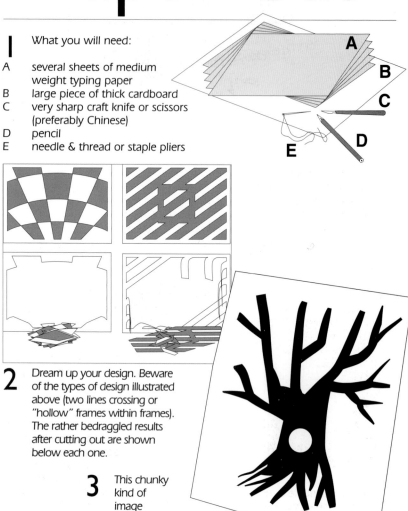

1 What you will need:

A several sheets of medium
weight typing paper
B large piece of thick cardboard
C very sharp craft knife or scissors
(preferably Chinese)
D pencil
E needle & thread or staple pliers

A
B
C
D
E

2 Dream up your design. Beware
of the types of design illustrated
above (two lines crossing or
"hollow" frames within frames).
The rather bedraggled results
after cutting out are shown
below each one.

3 This chunky
kind of
image
works much better.

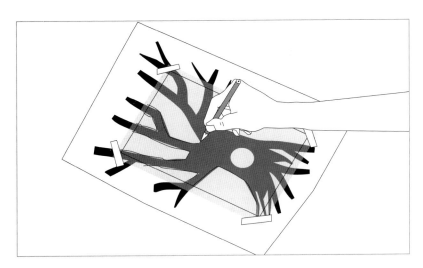

4 Trace the original drawing on to a sheet of typing paper and draw a frame around the outside.

5 Quickly scribble over the bits that you are going to cut out.

6 Now take as many sheets of typing paper as you require paper cuts and lightly stitch them together at the corners with the image on top. If you have access to staple pliers you may prefer to use them. You could also staple them to a board with a staple gun.

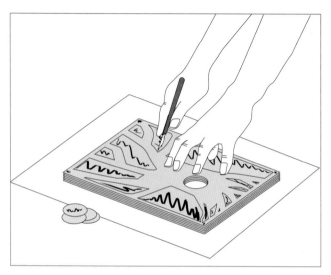

7 Place the sheets on a piece of cardboard on a solid, flat surface and cut through all the layers at once in order to remove the scribbled over section. You may like to tape down the edges with masking tape.

8 The paper cuts can be used singly or repetitively – perhaps taped over windows or unsympathetic fluorescent lights. **Do not use paper cuts near candles or electric lights that get hot!**

Paper cuts can be very large or very small, very simple or very intricate, single or multiple according to skill and taste. Chinese paper cuts, for example, have existed for over 1000 years and have been developed to a high level of craft.

Their use in funerals in the West is unusual but in our experience they offer something fragile and transitory which can be appropriate as either a gift of condolence or as a quick ceremonial decoration to improve unsympathetic environments such as crematoria. You can also try hanging them on a string.

THE FUNERAL

Paul Swift, Shipyard Worker

Lend us your black clip-on tie mate
I'm going to a funeral.
Yeah, the guy who died in the motorbike crash.
He was a cousin of our lass.
I don't like coming to funerals.
I choke up when I sing the hymns.
How come you know all the words?
Oh! You're a Catholic.
Thank you vicar. Very nice.
Look at that, a baby's dummy in the grass.
Funny thing, life.
Somebody goes. Somebody comes.

Suggested Structure
for a Ceremony

Here is a suggested structure to follow for those wishing to organise a funeral ceremony that is both dignified and formal, yet simple:

1 Arrival and Welcome:
opening words, including the name of the person whose life we are honouring. Mention and include the family/partners and their loss. The person (or preferably two) leading the ceremony may introduce themselves; outline their role; give an idea of the length of the ceremony; invite people to sit down and encourage people to move forward if it is a sparse gathering in a large venue; indicate anything particular that will happen during or after the ceremony.

2 Frame the Event:
some action or gesture to mark the start of the ceremony, eg someone lights a candle or lantern near the coffin.

3 Set the Mood:
listen to a piece of music; readings of prose and poetry with thoughts on the meaning and value of a life and the inevitability of death, chosen for their suitability to the person concerned (an old person dying at the end of a long and fulfilling life; a young adult killed in an accident; a child ...). The family may have suggested a favourite poem to be read. Everyone sings a secular song or a hymn together.

4 Tributes:
to the life of .... given by friends, relatives, colleagues. Readings, stories, poems, or something a family member has written, to be read on their behalf. This can be an opportunity to quote from letters of condolence that have already come in.

5 Committal:
Invite people to stand; indicate it is time for the final part of

the ceremony when we commit the body of .... to
its natural end. Offer a short silence for people's own thoughts
or prayers. If it is a crematorium, this is where curtains close
or the coffin glides out of sight. At the graveside this is the
lowering of the coffin into the ground. A handful of earth, or
flowers may be thrown into the grave.

6 Closing Words:
focussing people back onto their own lives, moving forward,
carrying this sorrow and loss. Thanks on behalf of the family
to those attending and for recent support given, where
appropriate. Final piece of music to listen to, or to sing
together.

7 Depart for Social Gathering.

Choosing the Right Words

The power of poetry

The words that we use at a funeral are incredibly important.
They are the means by which we can conjure up the essence of
the person who has died both to celebrate and mourn him or
her. Words also provide the channel for a sharing of deep and
complicated emotions. We may want to write a prose eulogy
describing the person and recalling particular characteristics,
memories or qualities that he or she possessed; we may select
special hymns or prayers that provide comfort; but if we want
to find words that convey the range of emotions that we are
experiencing – anger, despair, loss, grief, guilt, shock – then it
is probable that our best recourse is to turn to poetry.

Throughout time the job of the poet has been to find the
best words to illuminate the experience of life and to attempt
to make sense of things that most of us find too difficult
to encapsulate in words. A poem can say in a succinct and
memorable way what we might struggle and fail to express.
The right words can help us to grieve by deepening our
understanding of what has happened and the complex feelings
that have been evoked. The poet can speak on our behalf and
also remind us that, however alone we feel in our bereavement,
the loss of loved ones is part of the human experience.

Given the potential power of poetry, it is worth taking time to find the most significant poem or poems for the funeral. You may already have a favourite poem in mind, but there are several anthologies dedicated to death or bereavement and browsing through one of these will certainly reveal poems that resonate strongly with the emotions that you wish to convey. See **Resources and Contacts** for useful collections of poetry.

Eulogy

Memorials and funerals are ceremonies concerned with marking connections, as well as separation. They bring together friends, family and often wider more disparate groups of people, linking the living to the departed. The ceremony itself is a crucial part of that joining, within which the eulogy has pride of place. It is the moment at which the deceased is both brought close, and let go.

This explains why often giving a eulogy can be a difficult thing to do. The person speaking will feel a big sense of responsibility and have to cope with their own feelings. Yet the value of this act for the speaker and all those present cannot be over-estimated.

Services differ in their atmosphere, tradition, setting and tone; this 'formal' element can be trusted to carry a certain weight of the emotion. The eulogy must be specific, particular, even intimate and thereby seal the sense of occasion.

The secret of the eulogy's power is that it might move us to tears, but it can start to heal us too. It can help us to gain perspective, beginning the process of understanding that we cope with loss not by forgetting but by learning how best to live with our memories.

The eulogy is an expression of sorrow and a celebration of a life. As the words are spoken they give honour to the deceased. They give comfort by distilling the thoughts of the bereaved, asserting and dignifying our common humanity and the eventual destiny of us all.

Co-operative Funeralcare in collaboration with Poet Laureate Andrew Motion, produced in 2003 an inspiring and supportive booklet **Well Chosen Words – How to Write a Eulogy** available for free. See **Resources and Contacts**.

Music

How to find a Musician

1 If you would like to include live music in the funeral, decide what would be suitable and what you would like – discuss with others involved in arranging the funeral. We know of people using the following as solo instruments in several different services: flute ... 'cello ... jazz trumpet ... operatic tenor accordion ... classical guitar ... saxophone.

2 Unless you have a lot of money, time and technical support, avoid an arrangement which requires amplification. Everything in the above list was acoustic, and worked superbly.

3 Aim to stay local – find someone from within your region.

4 Contact any of the following for advice and information:

☐ Musicians' Union – London (020 7582 5566) www.musiciansunion.org.uk. For regional offices see **Resources and Contacts**.

☐ Regional Arts Boards – nine large regions around the country – contact the Music Officer, who may recommend you to a district arts association or arts development officer who should be able to help. See **Resources and Contacts**.

☐ Music teachers – via Yellow Pages (somewhere between Mushroom Growers and Nappy Delivery!)

☐ Music shops selling instruments (*not* hi-fi shops).

☐ Places of entertainment (check Yellow Pages): local theatre, arts centre, concert hall, civic hall – whoever programmes the music events and concerts may well know local instrumentalists.

☐ High Schools, Colleges, Music Schools, Universities – contact the Head of Music or Course Leader.

☐ Entertainers or Entertainment Agencies (Yellow Pages again) – you will have to sift carefully between bouncy castles, strippers and discos.

☐   Amateur societies (lists available from local libraries) putting
    on musical and operatic shows use 'semi-professional'
    orchestras with varying ensembles and will have a good list of
    contacts.

5   Contact the musician yourself – find out if they are interested
    and available and discuss what you had in mind, and why
    this seemed appropriate. Tell them about the person who has
    died. If you do not have strong feelings about which piece of
    music, ask them to make suggestions and talk this through.
    You may have to compromise, because you will be dependent
    on what pieces of music are in their repertoire or what they
    can get the sheet music for and reasonably learn in a very
    short time. Atmosphere of the music is the most important.
    You are most likely to be contracting a solo instrumentalist so
    that will limit the pieces available. Whereas a blues trumpeter
    is bound to know "Stormy Weather", the 'cellist may not
    know your favourite concerto.

6   Discuss and agree a fee for the job and how and when it is
    to be paid. You should expect to pay the Musicians' Union
    Grade 2 rate but do be aware that there will also be travel
    expenses if a journey over 15 miles is necessary.

7   Discuss travel arrangements and be precise about the time of
    the service and the address of the venue and any rehearsal.

8   Find out what the musician needs – a chair, a light – and
    where it should be. Ask the manager of the venue to provide
    this and if it is possible for the musician to be in a little
    early to get set up. Let the musician know, or give them the
    number, so they can sort this out for themselves, or even
    rehearse in the space.

9   Discuss what the musician will wear.

10 Finally, be absolutely clear about what you are asking them to
    do. Do they play throughout – on entry, during the service,
    on leaving or just have one solo? Make sure that whoever is
    leading the service knows about your plans for music, and
    make sure this person and the musician have a telephone
    number for each other, should they need to be in contact
    before the service.

WHAT IS THE LIFE OF A MAN?

collected from Harry Holman of Copthorne, Surrey

2
Did you not see the leaves but a short time ago?
They were all in full motion appearing to grow,
When the frost came upon them and wither'd them all,
Then the rain came upon them, and down they did fall.
3
If you go down to yonder churchyard, many names there you'll see,
Who have fallen from this world like the leaves from the trees;
What with age and affliction upon us all,
Like the leaves we shall wither and down we shall fall.

The Dead Good Funerals Book

Music: some suggestions

In the same way as many funerals are dreadful because we hand over our dead lives to experts who don't know us, who package us in the name of commerce, irrelevant religion and Victorian aesthetics, so it is with the music. We can have any music we want at our funerals but the chances are, that if we don't think about it beforehand, we'll end up with three 200 year old hymns (or probably two hymns if the crematorium's log-jammed with waiting hearses) advertising God, pitched two notes too high for the average congregation to sing well, written in old fashioned language, led by a priest who may enjoy singing, an organist with often a limited repertoire of hymns and classical tunes and an embarrassed congregation, unused to singing in public.

The preface to the well produced **Hymns Ancient and Modern** states that:

> "Christians have in their hearts a song, and hymns have been vehicles of the instinct for praise and worship by the congregation."

or as Tom Brown, the musicologist, puts it:

> "... the music element from sonorous passing bell to riotous hymn tugs the emotions and legitimises cathartic release."

Certainly standards such as Blake's "Jerusalem", Bunyan's "Who would true valour see", "Abide with me", "Psalm 23" (Crimond), "Love Divine, all loves excelling", "Amazing Grace", and "All things bright and beautiful", are good tunes worn into our consciousness from distant school assemblies. But they are all Christian and don't suit everyone. Other hymns such as "The Old Rugged Cross", still a favourite in Wesleyan areas or "Bringing in the Sheaves", and "When the Roll is called up Yonder" (both in Sankey and Moody) and "The Farewell Shanty", are alternatives but still Christian. Avoid modern evangelical hymns often written with three chords and containing the words "Jesus Saves", which are often musically dull and poetically weak.

As we indicate above, it can help to use live music with

different instruments rather than an organist. A solo flute, bagpipe, 'cello, violin, singer, or a small choir can transform a space. As the vicar usually has a contract with an organist (and "they are as hard as gold to find") if you want your own musician to play Fats Waller or Gershwin on or off the organ, you will need to negotiate very carefully and maybe have to pay for music and rehearsal time or find a new organist.

A shipyard worker I knew died recently, aged 43. We had both played brass in the same carnival street band. One evening after playing his trombone on a long parade he collapsed with a heart attack and died. In the crematorium service, packed with his work-mates and friends the shipyard silver band played some of his compositions and some traditional hymns. Outside at the end of the service five young musicians played carnival tunes in a lamenting New Orleans style. His poem "Funeral" appears in this book.

At Howard's funeral in the crematorium, The Beatles' "Here, There and Everywhere", was played on trumpet and at his memorial service in chapel a composition was written by Pete Moser for two voices, guitar and accordion. At many of the memorial services at St Paul's in Covent Garden (the Actors' Church) orchestras such as The BBC Big Band, or musicians (eg Larry Adler) have contributed. Trained musicians can be an enormous help. In our culture now (although we sing at football, or when drunk, at karaoke or in the bath) most white people find it hard to perform without rehearsal in a musty church when choked with emotion and looking down at the small print of half-remembered hymns. Even recorded music might be better.

If you do choose this option via a boogie box or the sound systems now available in most crematoria and some churches, check the sound levels in the space before the event. Simple music, such as a solo blues guitarist, can work better than complex orchestrations or heavy percussion which may reverberate with too much echo and go mushy. Recordings of black gospel choirs might work if they can be loud enough but of course the real thing would be much better.

Churches are, quite understandably, wary of secular music (although a clerical friend of mine recounts with glee the memorial service he conducted for a drag artist with an outrageous soundtrack of "Someday my Prince will

Come"). But normally it may be easier to pick your own accompaniment if you opt for a ceremony in a neutral space such as a crematorium, a village hall, a town hall, a private house, a studio theatre, an art gallery or in a garden.

Once we abandon religious hymns and organ there is no limit. Most people are familiar with a great deal of music and will know instinctively what to pick. Dvorjak's "New World Symphony" (with the words "Coming Home, Coming Home"), Bach's "Fantasia in G Minor", "Ferry across the Mersey", "Yesterday", "Sailing", "The Carnival is Over", Edith Piaf's "No Regrets", Nina Simone, anything from Sweet Honey in the Rock, particularly "Your Children are not Your Children" (from Ghibran) and unfortunately "My Way", could work if that's your taste and it's shared by the congregation.

Browsing through a CD collection to select your own funeral choice need not be morbid. A good way in would be the **Rough Guide to World Music** published in 1994. This is a complete handbook to music played by four-fifths of the world; perfect if you fancy breaking convention with anything from Cajun to Calypso or wonderful songs from Asian, African and Central European traditions. Indeed discovering the right music for your funeral could be a lifetime's work ...

There is currently a shortage of secular hymns. "What is the Life of a Man?", reproduced here, is a good one (it was introduced to us by Peter Stark and Tom Brown). I am told that Dave Webber's "Parting Song" is beginning to be used. As is Richard Thompson's rock anthem "Meet on the Ledge" (recorded by Fairport Convention) and probably Eric Clapton's "Tears in Heaven", Jan Garbarek's "Officium" with the Hilliard Ensemble (ECM Records) fuses lyrical modern Jazz and Gregorian chant and could be perfect. Choose whatever works for you, the deceased, and the rest of the congregation together. Be aware though that in moments of trauma it is easy to offend. When different tribes of varying ages and tastes meet, people may have little in common. Death is hard enough to deal with without wasting emotion. Grandma might prefer Elvis to John Wesley, but don't bank on it.

Finally a note about processions and singing. Roman funeral ceremonies took place at night. Our word funeral was derived from "funales" – the fire torches carried in procession. Like processions, three hundred years ago singing was also common en route to Church and Church to grave.

There is a story in Neal's **History of the Puritans** that:

> "Mr Cradley, who was the intruding minister at Cripplegate Church, seeing a corpse being borne for burial there, attended by singing clerks in their surplices, threatened to shut the doors against them. The singing men, however, resisted resolving to go through with their work till the Alderman's deputy threatened to lay them by the heels for breaking the peace."

Curiously, until about one hundred years ago, this tradition of choral funeral procession survived around Ulverston in Furness. As this is where Welfare State International is now based we may be able to revive the idea or even use percussion bands to mark the occasion. Always presuming it doesn't interfere with the previous service; that local cemetery by-laws permit; and that "noise pollution" law is not invoked. At death today the Alderman's Deputy has become the Environmental Health Officer with decibel meter. He may eliminate the sonorous bell. But not the silent scythe.

Hymns are sung prayers

Again, if you wish to choose your own prayers it is worth researching in advance. One or two of the poems in this book may be suitable and the BHA, in their excellent book **Funerals without God**, indicate a number of useful prose readings and over twenty appropriate poems from authors as diverse as Rossetti, Swinburne, Shakespeare, R L Stevenson, Kipling, Samuel Butler, Hardy and Shelley. As the Humanists point out – officiants tend to build up their own collections and on occasion the favourite writings of the deceased are also selected. Whichever readings you choose, however, it is worth ensuring that the reader is confident and possibly rehearsed in the space chosen for the ceremony.

In November 1995 "Do not stand at my grave" – found in the papers of a soldier killed in Northern Ireland – became the

THE JOY OF LIVING

Lyrics by Ewan MacColl

Farewell, you northern hills, you mountains all goodbye
Moorlands and stony ridges, crags and peaks, goodbye
Glyder Fach farewell, cold big Scafell, cloud-bearing Suilven
Sun-warmed rocks and the cold of Bleaklow's frozen sea
The snow and the wind and the rain of hills and mountains
Days in the sun and the tempered wind and the air like wine
And you drink and you drink till you're drunk on the joy of living

Farewell to you, my love, my time is almost done
Lie in my arms once more until the darkness comes
You filled all my days, held the night at bay, dearest companion
Years pass by and they're gone with the speed of birds in flight
Our lives like the verse of a song heard in the mountains
Give me your hand and love and join your voice with mine
And we'll sing of the hurt and the pain and the joy of living

Take me to some high place of heather, rock and ling
Scatter my dust and ashes, feed me to the wind
So that I may be part of all you see, the air you are breathing
I'll be part of the curlew's cry and the soaring hawk,
The blue milkwort and the sundew hung with diamonds
I'll be riding the gentle breeze as it blows through your hair
Reminding you how we shared in the joy of living

The Joy of Living
Traditional Sicilian tune, words written by Ewan MacColl
Ewan MacColl and Peggy Seeger
Black and White – Ewan MacColl – The Definitive Collection

most popular poem broadcast in Britain for nearly 60 years. Some of its words have been traced to a Native American tradition and it was used at a memorial service on the twenty-fifth anniversary of the death of Marilyn Monroe in 1987.

> Do not stand at my grave and weep;
> I am not there. I do not sleep.
> I am a thousand winds that blow.
> I am the diamond glints on the snow.
> I am the gentle autumn's rain.
> When you awaken in the morning's hush,
> I am the swift uplifting rush
> Of quiet birds in circled flight.
> I am the soft stars that shine at night.
> Do not stand at my grave and cry;
> I am not there. I did not die.

Originally broadcast on BBC2's **Bookworm** programme, it generated 10,000 requests for free copies (many from bereaved people); £6,000 for the "Children in Need" appeal and a new single by Bros!

What a Celebratory Artist can offer

Involving professional artists in the creation of a funeral can contribute to the sense of occasion and celebration. Many artists are used to working in community situations and welcome the opportunity to use their skills within the context of a significant event. You might consider commissioning a special piece of music or sculpture, or inviting an artist to work with you to transform the space or make artefacts and imagery that will convey something of the essence of the person whose life is being marked. Examples of work that artists have done in the past:

■ Decorating a route for a processional arrival with flags or banners.

■ Using new technologies to create a visual record of a person's life.

■ Making lanterns and other symbolic objects.

Artists have the capacity to fulfil your wildest dreams and to exceed them in the most wonderful way. An open and exploratory conversation as early as possible is recommended.

Commissioning an Artist to Paint a Coffin

This is a subjective process and requires time and negotiation to be clear about expectations on both sides. Commissioning an artist to paint a coffin is most suited to those with some time to plan ahead, such as: the relatives of an old person who has expressed an interest in such a coffin; someone who has been given the diagnosis of a terminal illness and intends to participate in the planning of their own funeral; someone in good health who decides to take such a step and store the decorated coffin until it is needed.

It is best to look for an artist in your region, whose work you admire. Not all artists would feel able to tackle such a job. Artists who work on a bold scale usually feel more confident. Check that they have a studio or workspace big enough to receive the coffin, preferably on the ground floor. Consider size of doorways and staircases. Expect to pay a minimum fee of £500-£600 to a lesser-known artist for a personal commission, in addition to the purchase price of the coffin, plus delivery and collection. You may wish to commission an artist with a reputation, in which case expect to pay several times the above, and expect to wait for some months.

The artist should be asked to paint the underneath of the coffin too, however simply, as this could be visible when the coffin is carried. Collage, or addition of flammable materials and mouldings on the outside will not be permitted by the authorities, on account of the technical processes surrounding burial, natural burial and cremation. The finished coffin has to be suitable for handling in the traditional fashion, lowering on straps into the grave; sliding along rollers in and out of the hearse; or into the cremator. Deciding how to paint the coffin is the hardest part. Some people have very clear ideas, but often the final design is the outcome of conversations and listening between the artist and the client. How to find a visual artist? Arts Council England regional offices, galleries, art and design colleges, societies of artists.

RESOURCES AND CONTACTS

Information

The Natural Death Centre
6 Blackstock Mews
Blackstock Road
London
N4 2BT
020 7359 8391
ndc@alberyfoundation.org   www.naturaldeath.org.uk
Provides information to those wishing to organise funerals with or without the help of funeral directors. Many excellent publications, including handbook, information pack, death plan, advance funeral wishes, forms and Living Will forms. Initiates research projects and gatherings to discuss death and dying.

The Office of Fair Trading Report on the Funerals Industry 2000
The site also provides consumer information on your rights when organising or buying a prepaid funeral.
www.oft.gov.uk

Oddfellows Report on Funerals
UK Funerals Online
www.uk-funerals.co.uk

Charter for the Bereaved
Available from Institute of Cemetery and Crematorium Management, free download and other details about work they do.
ICCM National Office
City of London Cemetery
Aldersbrook Road
Manor Park
London E12 5DQ.
020 8989 4661
www.iccm-uk.com

Low Price Funerals
Practical and informative site by UK funeral director attempting to build network of low-cost funeral providers.
www.lowpricefunerals.co.uk

Department for Work and Pensions
General information on benefits which can be accessed by the bereaved.
www.dwp.gov.uk/lifeevent/benefits/

London Borough of Richmond Cemeteries
The Cemetery Office
East Sheen Cemetery
Sheen Road
Richmond
TW10 5BJ
020 8876 4511
cemeteries@richmond.gov.uk   www.richmond.gov.uk/cemeteries

Help the Hospices
Hospice House
34-44 Britannia Street
London
WC1X 9JG
020 7520 8200
www.helpthehospices.org.uk

British Humanist Association
1 Gower Street
London
WC1E 6HD
020 7079 3580
info@humanism.org.uk   www.humanism.org.uk
National network of funeral officiants, training opportunities.

SANDS (Stillbirth and Neonatal Death Society)
c/o 33 Hawk Close
Abbeydale
Gloucester
GL4 4WE
01452 533778

Age Concern
0800 009966
www.ageconcern.org.uk
Find regional branches in your local phone book.

Arts Council England
0845 300 6200
Phone for regional offices.

Scottish Arts Council
0845 603 6000

Arts Council Wales
029 2037 6500

Musicians' Union
60-62 Clapham Road
London
SW9 OJJ
020 7582 5566
Phone for regional offices.

Specialist Services

Bristol Memorial Woodlands
Earthcott Green
Alveston
Bristol
BS35 3TA
www.memorialwoodlands.com
01454 414999

Memorials By Artists
Snape Priory
Snape
Suffolk
IP17 1SA
01728 688934
harriet@memorialartscharity.org.uk
www.memorialsbyartists.co.uk
Contemporary stone memorials: design and fine lettering.

The Stile Company
The Leggett
Thatcher's Close
Epwell
Banbury
Oxfordshire
OX15 6LJ
01295 780372
info@the-stile.co.uk
www.the-stile.co.uk
The Stile Company has been formed to assist people who want to

install their own unique features in places that are special to them
– whether a crafted stile or seat, a sculpture, a sundial, a stone wall,
a tree – especially to mark an event such as a death, memorial, birth
or wedding.

The Woodland & Wildlife Conservation Company Ltd
Birch Hall Farm
Coppice Row
Theydon Bois
Essex
CM16 7DR
01992 814909
enquiries@woodlandandwildlife.co.uk
www.woodlandandwildlife.co.uk

Suppliers

ARKA Original Funerals and Ecopod Coffins
39-41 Surrey Street
Brighton
BN1 3PB
01273 766620
www.eco-funerals.com   info@eco-funerals.com

Compakta Ltd
Environ
Parkfield
Western Park
Hinckley Road
Leicester
LE3 6HX
01162 333566
www.eco-coffin.co.uk
*Compakta cardboard coffins, dappled white, inset lid, ideal for
painting. Arrive ready assembled, overnight delivery if required.*

Eco-Coffins.com
Channel Business Centre
Castle Hill Avenue
Folkestone
CT20 2RD
01303 850856
www.eco-coffins.com
Simple pine coffins in solid wood from sustainable forests, modest prices.

Ecopartnerships
Mill Street Studios
Donald Boddy
PO Box 2287
Bridgnorth
WV15 5YE
01746 761537
info@ecopartnerships.com
Ecopartnerships offer extensive consultancy planning and design
services to landowners and local authorities who wish to create
alternative burial sites.

Engrefco
Alterchrome House
Murray Road
Orpington
BR5 3QY
0800 018877
They sell a new design of cardboard coffin pictured on p89.

The Green Burial Company plc
Olney Green Burial Ground
Yardley Road
Olney
MK46 5EH
01234 241808
information@thegreenburialcompany.plc.uk

Green Endings Funerals Ltd
141 Fortess Road
London
NW5 2HR
020 7424 0345
info@greenendings.co.uk   www.greenendings.co.uk
Roslyn Cassidy, Director.

green fuse
The Old Stables
Station Road
Totnes
Devon
TQ9 5HW
01803 840779
www.greenfuse.co.uk   greenfuse@lineone.net
Ceremony and celebration with professional floristry services.

Green Undertakings Ltd
Hampden House
Rosliston Road
Burton on Trent
DE15 9RA
01283 540009
info@greenundertakings.co.uk   www.greenundertakings.co.uk

PB (UK)
Triangle House
62 Victoria Road
Cirencester
GL7 1ES
01285 653298
ecocoffinpbuk@hotmail.com
*Supply the 'Peace Box' – wood-grain cardboard coffin, gabled lid,
good for painting.*

The SAWD Partnership
Highsted Farm
Highsted Valley
Sittingbourne
ME9 0AG
01795 472262
www.bamboocoffins.cjb.net
Sell handmade biodegradable bamboo Eco Coffins.

Vic Fearn Company Ltd
Coffin Makers, Crabtree Mill, Hempshill Lane, Bulwell,
Nottingham
NG6 8PF
0115 927 1907
*Stocks range of coffins, some simple and elegant, some unusual and
artist-designed. Also recycled timber and green coffins. Can build to
order at short notice.*

Willow Coffins
Linden Spinney
Chagford
Devon
TQ13 8JF
01647 432451
nigel@willowcoffins.co.uk   www.willowcoffins.co.uk
*Makers of woven willow coffins from willow harvested in
Sedgemoor, Somerset.*

Zimbabwean Collapsible Coffin Company
71b Shakespeare Road,
London
SE24 0LA
Tel: 0207 1326 0274

Training

Australian & International College of Celebrancy
www.collegeofcelebrancy.com   afcc@netspace.net.au
0061 3 9428 9926

National Funerals College
Leyton House
Warwick Road
Bristol
BS6 6HE
0117 973 0045
malcolm.johnson@bristol.ac.uk

Welfare State International
Lanternhouse
The Ellers
Ulverston
Cumbria
LA12 0AA
01229 581127
www.welfare-state.org   info@welfare-state.com

Books

Natural Death Handbook
A mine of practical and helpful information and addresses.
Rider Books New Edition November 2004

Ceremonies for Life
Michael Jordan
Collins & Brown 2001

Dancing on the Grave
Nigel Barley
Abacus 1997

Deeply Into the Bone: Re-inventing Rites of Passage
Ronald L. Grimes
University of California Press 2002

Do Not Go Gentle: Poems for Funerals
Editor – Neil Astley
Bloodaxe Books 2003

From Beginning to End
Robert Fulghum
Fawcett Books 1997

Funerals and How to Improve Them
Dr Tony Walter
Hodder & Stoughton (1990)
Currently out of print

Funerals Without God
Jane Wynne Willson
British Humanist Association

Generations
Editors – Melanie Hart and James Loader
Penguin Books 1998

Going into Darkness: Fantastic Coffins from Africa
Thierry Secretan
Thames & Hudson 1995

Passages of the Soul
James Roose-Evans
Vega Books 2002
Particularly Chapter 8: 'The Making of a Ritual'.

Preparing for Approaching Death
Article containing detailed description of the final stages of dying, designed to inform family, friends and carers and those facing death. Available for free download.
Produced by the North Central Florida Hospice
Hospice Net
Suite 51
401 Bowling Avenue
Nashville, TN 37205-5124
United States of America
www.hospicenet.org

Rites and Ceremonies: A Practical Guide to Alternative Funerals
Kate Gordon
Constable & Robinson, 1999

Seasons of Life
Editor Nigel Collins
Rationalist Press Association

Staying Alive: Real Poems for Unreal Times
Editor: Neil Astley
Bloodaxe Books 2002

The Denial of Death
Ernest Becker
Free Press 1985

The Long Pale Corridor: Contemporary Poems of Bereavement
Editors – Judi Benson, Agneta Falk
Bloodaxe Books 1996

The Tibetan Book of Living and Dying
Sogyal Rinpoche
Rider 2002

Vigor Mortis: the end of the Death Taboo
Kate Berridge
Profile Books Ltd 2001

Well Chosen Words – How to Write a Eulogy
Booklet – available for free.
Co-operative Funeralcare
www.funeralcare.co-op.co.uk
0800 083 6301

INDEX